Ready-to-Use

SOCIAL SKILLS
LESSONS &
ACTIVITIES
for Grades 1-3

RUTH WELTMANN BEGUN, Editor

A ready-to-use curriculum based on real-life situations to help you
build children's self-esteem, self-control, respect for the
rights of others, and a sense of responsibility for one's own actions.

JOSSEY-BASS
A Wiley Imprint
www.josseybass.com

Published by Jossey-Bass
A Wiley Imprint
989 Market Street, San Francisco, CA 94103-1741   www.josseybass.com

Jossey-Bass books and products are available through most bookstores. To contact Jossey-Bass directly
call our Customer Care Department within the U.S. at 800-956-7739, outside the U.S. at 317-572-3986
or fax 317-572-4002.

Jossey-Bass also publishes its books in a variety of electronic formats. Some content that appears in
print may not be available in electronic books.

Library of Congress Cataloging-in-Publication Data
Ready-to-use social skills lessons & activities for grades 1–3
   Ruth Weltmann Begun, editor ; The Society for Prevention of Violence with
The Center for Applied Research in Education
         p.   cm.—(Social skills curriculum activities library)
      Includes bibliographical references.
      ISBN 0-87628-864-6 (Spiral)   ISBN 0-87628-473-X (Paper)
      1. Social skills—Study and teaching (Elementary)—Activity
programs.   2. Social skills—Study and teaching (Elementary)—
Outlines, syllabi, etc.   3. Social skills in children.   I. Begun,
Ruth Weltmann.   II. Society for Prevention of Violence (Ohio)
III. Center for Applied Research in Education.   IV. Series.
HQ783.R39   1995   95-24335
646.7'0083'4—dc20

FIRST EDITION
PB Printing 10 9 8

ABOUT THIS SOCIAL SKILLS TEACHING RESOURCE

Today's educators carry added responsibilities because significant social changes have had an impact on human relations. Family ties have been loosened. The number of single-parent families has grown. Stresses in many families are often high. Thus, youngsters are frequently exposed to influences which tend to make them aggressive and possibly violent. Moreover, television, now in almost every home, frequently shows events not suitable for guiding children. Youngsters who cannot read and write watch violent scenes and might draw wrong conclusions. Unless schools, daycare centers, head start programs, and parents counteract asocial influences starting at the pre-kindergarten level, verbal and physical interpersonal abuse and violence will be an increasing problem.

This resource is one of four books in the "Social Skills Curriculum Activities Library," a practical series designed to help teachers, care givers and parents in giving children regular social skills lessons. The full Library spans all grade levels, preschool through grade 12, and includes:

READY-TO-USE SOCIAL SKILLS LESSONS & ACTIVITIES FOR GRADES PreK–K
READY-TO-USE SOCIAL SKILLS LESSONS & ACTIVITIES FOR GRADES 1–3
READY-TO-USE SOCIAL SKILLS LESSONS & ACTIVITIES FOR GRADES 4–6
READY-TO-USE SOCIAL SKILLS LESSONS & ACTIVITIES FOR GRADES 7–12

Each grade-level book provides 50 or more detailed, age-appropriate lessons for developing specific social skills accompanied by reproducible activity sheets and other activities to help students learn the skill. The lessons are presented in a uniform format and follow a Structured Learning approach to teach the skills. They focus on real situations in children's own lives, such as dealing with feelings and peer pressure, and are readily adapted for use in any classroom, school, or home setting.

The lessons and activities in Books 1, 2 and 3 are followed by two special sections entitled "Social Skills Task Review" and "Social Skills Family Training Booklet." "Social Skills Task Review" presents 21 social skills topics that can be used for teacher-led discussions during Circle Time. These are printed in the form of discussion cards which can be photocopied and cut out for use at the appropriate time. You can introduce each topic once before studying a skill and later, following the lesson, to measure what children have learned. The Social Skills Family Training Booklet is addressed to parents and single pages can be copied as needed for use with individual children. The booklet includes a brief introduction to its purposes and acknowledgment to its originators followed by a family social skills checklist, and helpful hints and reminders for using the booklet and teaching social skills effectively. The heart of the booklet is comprised of "Fourteen Selected Social Skills" with suggested skill activities that can be done within the family.

NOTE: Copies of the booklet can be ordered from the publisher, The Center for Applied Research in Education, at the minimum quantity of 20.

Most of the lessons and activities in the Social Skills Library were written, edited, and class-room-tested by teachers from the Cleveland (Ohio) Public Schools in cooperation with faculty from John Carroll University's Department of Education. The project was funded by The Society for Prevention of Violence (SPV), a non-profit organization founded by S.J. Begun, Ph.D., and his wife Ruth Weltmann Begun, M.S., and sponsored by them and various contributing corporations and foundations. Many individual members of the SPV also made substantial contributions. Specific credits are given on the Acknowledgments page.

Major objectives of teaching these lessons are to build students' self-esteem, self-control, respect for the rights of others, and a sense of responsibility for one's own actions. Another objective is to teach the students to settle grievances and conflicts through communication without recourse to violence. We believe that such training can be effective and successful by increasing discipline and reducing the drop-out rate. Thus, students will benefit from social skills training throughout their lives.

S.J. Begun, Ph.D.

Ruth Weltmann Begun, M.S.

The Society for Prevention of Violence

THE SOCIAL SKILLS SONG
(Tune: "Mary Had a Little Lamb")

WE CAN USE OUR SOCIAL SKILLS
SOCIAL SKILLS, SOCIAL SKILLS
WE CAN USE OUR SOCIAL SKILLS
AS WE SPREAD OUR GOOD WILL

EVERY DAY IN EVERY WAY
EVERY WAY, EVERY WAY
EVERY DAY IN EVERY WAY
OUR CHARACTER WE BUILD

ACKNOWLEDGMENTS

The Founders, Trustees, Members, Friends of the Society for Prevention of Violence (SPV), and many foundations and corporations sponsored the writing of the social skills training material in the "Social Skills Curriculum Activities Library" with the objectives of reducing interpersonal violence and solving controversies in an amicable way.

Credit for writing the PreK-K lessons and activities in Volume 1 in the Library belongs to a collective effort by a group of teachers and administrators of the Cleveland (Ohio) Public Schools who had unique experience in teaching pre-kindergarten and kindergarten children. They wrote under the direction of four professors from the Department of Education of the John Carroll University in Cleveland, Ohio, assisted by consultants of the Society for Prevention of Violence (SPV). The concept of a curriculum was initiated by the then Executive Director of SPV, Ruth Weltmann Begun, who did the final page collection and editing of the finished manuscripts for the Curriculum.

ABOUT THE SOCIETY FOR PREVENTION OF VIOLENCE (SPV)

The Society for Prevention of Violence (SPV) is dedicated to reducing the prevalence of violent acts and asocial behaviors in children and adults through education. It accomplishes this mission by teaching children and adults the use of the skills necessary to build their character, helping them acquire a strong values system, motivating them to develop their communication skills and to realize growth in interpersonal relationships. The mission includes integration of social and academic skills to encourage those who use them to reach their full potential and contribute to our nation's society by being able to make decisions and solve problems through effective and appropriate means.

As a non-profit organization, the Society had its origin in 1972 as The Begun Institute for The Study of Violence and Aggression at John Carroll University (Cleveland, Ohio). A multitude of information was gathered, studied, and analyzed during the ensuing ten-year period. Symposia were held which involved numerous well-known presenters and participants from various career fields. Early on, the founders of the Institute, S.J. and Ruth Begun, foresaw the trend of increasing violence in our families, communities and across the nation, and chose to take a leadership role in pioneering an educational approach to help alleviate aggressive and antisocial behavior. The educational approach was and continues to be the sole <u>PROACTIVE</u> means to change behaviors. Current conditions reflect our society's reliance on reactive means of dealing with this problem. During the next ten-year period, through the determination and hard work of Ruth Weltmann Begun as executive director, the workshops, parent training sessions, collaborative projects, and a comprehensive (preschool through grade 12) Social Skills Training Curriculum were developed.

Today, classroom teachers in numerous school districts across the country are utilizing this internationally recognized curriculum. The Society continually seeks support through individual donors, grants, direct paid services, and material/consultant service sales. It also has expanded its involvement in the educational process by:

- publishing a semiannual newsletter and other pertinent articles;
- providing in-service training for professional staffs, parents, and others;
- providing assistance in resource identification, proposal writing/project design and evaluation;
- tailoring instructional (academic and other) delivery designs to specific school/organization needs; and
- implementing pilot demonstration projects with foundation support.

As we move into and through the twenty-first century, we must work diligently and cooperatively to turn challenges into success.

The Society also offers graduate-level workshops in cooperation with John Carroll University for educators. Credits earned in these workshops may be applied toward renewal of certificates through the Ohio Department of Education.

For further information, contact The Society for Prevention of Violence, 3439 West Brainard Road #102, Woodmere, Ohio 44122 (phone 216/591-1876) or 3109 Mayfield Road, Cleveland Heights, Ohio 44118 (phone 216/371-5545).

ABOUT THE SOCIAL SKILLS CURRICULUM

Philosophy

We believe that the learning of social skills is the foundation for social and academic adequacy. It assists in the prevention of social problems and leads to successful functioning and survival skills for our citizens. Social behavior and academic behavior are highly correlated. We believe it is more productive to teach children the proper ways to behave than to admonish them for improper behavior. This requires direct and systematic teaching, taking into consideration social and developmental theory in the affective, cognitive, and psycho-motor domains. Learning should be sequential, linked to community goals, and consistent with behaviors which are relevant to student needs. This social skills curriculum is based on these beliefs.

Curriculum Overview

As children grow, one way they learn social behaviors is by watching and interacting with other people. Some children who have failed to learn appropriate behaviors have lacked opportunities to imitate good role models, have received insufficient or inappropriate reinforcement, or have misunderstood adequate social experiences.

The Social Skills Curriculum is designed to teach these behaviors in ways that correlate with child development theory, namely how children learn in their natural environment. Each lesson provides models for children to imitate and correction strategies following practice of the skills. The teacher and the rest of the class then provide positive reinforcement to encourage the continued use of the appropriate skills in situations that occur in any environment.

Teachers using this curriculum can be flexible. The curriculum is designed to be used in the classroom as lessons taught for about 20-30 minutes, two to three times a week. However, it is not the intent that these be the only times social skills are taught and learned. Every opportunity should be used to reinforce, model, and coach the children so that they can practice the skills enough to feel comfortable with them as part of their ways of behaving. Therefore, the teacher should remind the students of the skills and the need to use them in all appropriate situations once the skills have been demonstrated. The teacher should also plan to model the skills in any and all interactions with the children. The teacher should be *consistent* in not only using the skills when they are taught, but in using them in all interactions with the students. Only this kind of consistent modeling will assure that the children will see the skills used repeatedly and begin to know and feel comfortable with using them. Teachers should also feel free to adapt the material to class needs and to design and develop strategies, models, and interventions other than those suggested here. Students can even be involved in helping to think of modeling strategies and other techniques.

The Social Skills Curriculum Library is graded pre-Kindergarten through Grade Twelve and presented in four volumes focusing on four different levels: grades preK-K, 1-3, 4-6, and 7-12. It uses a structured learning approach to teach the skills. *Structured Learning* is a holistic teaching method that provides a framework for systematic teaching in a way that is similar to academics. The emphasis in this curriculum is to provide constructive and structured behaviors for socially skill-deficient children.

Structured Learning consists of *four basic components:* modeling, role playing, discussion of performance, and use in real-life situations. For more effective teaching, the lessons include eight steps that follow a directed lesson format (see below):

Social Skill: A social behavior that is directly observable.

Behavioral Objective: An expected outcome of learning the social skill that can be evaluated.

Directed Lesson: Each behavior is defined and stated in observable terms; the behavior is demonstrated and practiced; a student's level of performance is evaluated and inappropriate behaviors are corrected. Positive reinforcement is used to encourage continued use of the skill in all areas of the student's environment.

1. ***Establish the Need:*** The purpose of teaching the lesson is included. What benefits will learning the skill provide? What are the consequences of not learning the behavior?

2. ***Introduction:*** Stories, poems, puppets, and questions are used to make the social skill more concrete to the children.

3. ***Identify the Skill Components:*** These skill steps are used to teach the behavior. By following and practicing these steps, the students will be able to demonstrate the behavior when needed.

4. ***Model the Skill:*** The teacher or socially adept child demonstrates the appropriate behaviors so that the students can imitate them. The skill components are referred to during the modeling.

5. ***Behavioral Rehearsal:*** The children are given an opportunity to perform the behavior which can be evaluated, corrected, and reinforced.

   A. Selection—The teacher selects participants or asks for volunteers. The number of children depends on the time allowed and whatever is appropriate for each lesson.

   B. Role Play—The participants are assigned their roles or situations they will role play.

   C. Completion—This is a means to determine that the role playing is complete. After each role play, reinforce correct behaviors, identify inappropriate behaviors, and reenact role play with corrections. If there are no corrections, role play is complete.

   D. Reinforcers—Positive reinforcement by the teacher and the class is used for maintenance of the skill. Various methods can be used: verbal encouragement, tangible rewards, special privileges, and keeping a record of social and academic improvement.

   E. Discussion—The student's level of performance is evaluated and inappropriate behaviors are corrected. How did the participants feel while performing? What difficulties might be faced in implementing the skill? What observations did the class make?

6. ***Practice:*** Activities that help the children summarize the skill. The practice can be done by using worksheets, doing art projects, making film strips, writing stories, keeping diaries and charts, and so on.

7. ***Independent Use:*** Activities that help facilitate the use of these behaviors outside the school environment. Family and friends take an active role in reinforcing the importance of using these alternative behaviors in a conflict situation.

8. ***Continuation:*** At the end of each lesson, the teacher reminds the class that applying social skills can benefit them in academic and social relationships. Stress that although there are difficulties in applying the skills (such as in regard to negative peer pressure), the benefits outweigh the problems. One such benefit is more self-confidence in decision-making. Maintaining social behavior is an ongoing process. It requires teachers to show appropriate behaviors and reinforce them when they are demonstrated.

STRUCTURED LEARNING

FOUR BASIC COMPONENTS

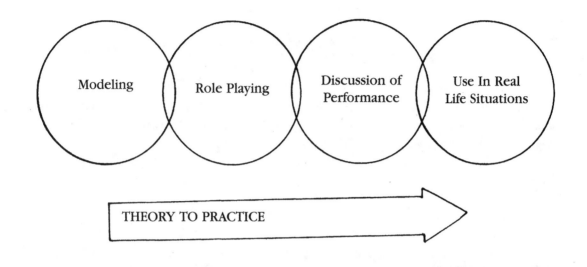

| Modeling | Role Playing | Discussion of Performance | Use In Real Life Situations |

THEORY TO PRACTICE

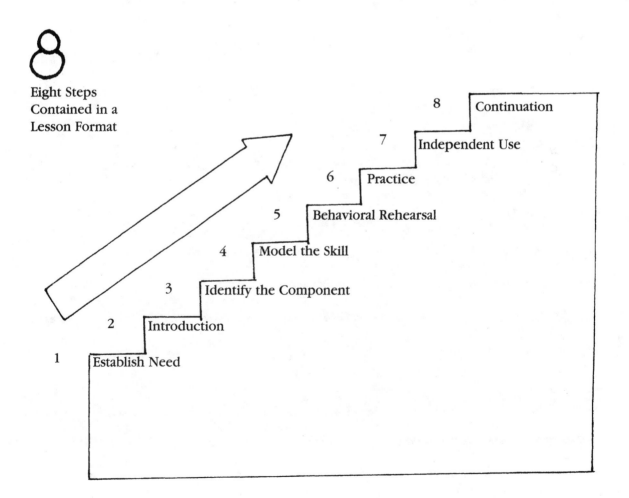

Eight Steps Contained in a Lesson Format

8 Continuation
7 Independent Use
6 Practice
5 Behavioral Rehearsal
4 Model the Skill
3 Identify the Component
2 Introduction
1 Establish Need

BIBLIOGRAPHY

Books

Apter, Stephen J., and Arnold P. Goldstein. *Youth Violence: Program and Prospects.* Needham Heights, MA: Allyn & Bacon, 1986.

Ballare, Antonia, and Angelique Lampros. *Behavior Smart! Ready-to-Use Activities for Building Personal and Social Skills for Grades K-4.* West Nyack, NY: Center for Applied Research in Education, 1994.

Cartledge, Gwendolyn, and Joanne Fellows Milburn. *Teaching Social Skills to Children,* 2nd ed. Needham Heights, MA: Allyn & Bacon, 1986.

Cherry, Clare. *Please Don't Sit on the Kids: Alternatives to Punitive Discipline.* Belmont, CA: Fearon-Pitman, 1982.

Chirinian, Helene. *Cartoon Comprehension.* Redondo Beach, CA: Frank Schaeffer Publications, 1980.

Eberle, Bob. *Help! in Managing Your Classroom.* Carthage, IL: Good Apple, 1984.

Farnette, C., I Forte, and B. Loss. *I've Got Me and I'm Glad,* rev. ed. Nashville, TN: Incentive Publications, 1989.

Feshbach, Norma, and Seymour Feshbach et al. *Learning to Care: Classroom Activities for Social and Affective Development.* Glenview, IL: Good Year Books, 1983.

Ginott, Haim G. *Teacher and Child: A Book for Parents.* New York: Macmillan, 1984.

Goldstein, Arnold P., Stephen J. Apter, and Berj Harootunian. *School Violence.* Englewood Cliffs, NJ: Prentice Hall, 1984.

Goldstein, Arnold P. et al. *Skillstreaming the Adolescent: A Structured Learning Approach to Teaching Prosocial Skills.* Champaign, IL: Research Press, 1980.

Grevious, Saundrah Clark. *Ready-to-Use Multicultural Activities for Primary Children.* West Nyack, NY: Center for Applied Research in Education, 1993.

Kaplan, P.G., S.K. Crawford, and S.L. Nelson. *Nice.* Denver: Love, 1977.

Mannix, Darlene. *Be a Better Student: Lessons and Worksheets for Teaching Behavior Management in Grades 4-9.* West Nyack, NY: Center for Applied Research in Education, 1989.

_____. *Life Skills Activities for Special Children.* West Nyack, NY: Center for Applied Research in Education, 1991.

_____. *Social Skills Activities for Special Children.* West Nyack, NY: Center for Applied Research in Education, 1993.

McElmurry, Mary Ann. *Caring.* Carthage, IL: Good Apple, 1981.

_____. *Feelings.* Carthage, IL: Good Apple, 1981.

McGinnis, Ellen, and Arnold P. Goldstein. *Skillstreaming the Elementary School Child: A Guide for Teaching Prosocial Skills.* Champaign, IL: Research Press, 1984.

Schwartz, Linda. *The Month-to-Month Me.* Santa Barbara, CA: The Learning Works, 1976.

Standish, Bob. *Connecting Rainbows.* Carthage, IL: Good Apple, 1982.

Stephens, Thomas M. *Social Skills in the Classroom,* 2nd ed. Lutz, FL: Psychological Assessment Resources, 1992.

Stull, Elizabeth Crosby. *Multicultural Discovery Activities for the Elementary Grades.* West Nyack, NY: Center for Applied Research in Education, 1994.

Teolis, Beth. *Ready-to-Use Self-Esteem Activities for Grades 4–8.* West Nyack, NY: Center for Applied Research in Education, 1995.

Toner, Patricia Rizzo. *Relationships and Communication Activities.* West Nyack, NY: Center for Applied Research in Education, 1993.

_____. *Stress Management and Self-Esteem Activities.* West Nyack, NY: Center for Applied Research in Education, 1993.

Documents

Early Identification of Classification of Juvenile Delinquents: Hearing Before the Subcommittee of the Committee on the Constitution, U.S. Senate, 97th Congress; Serial No. J-97-70; October 22, 1981; Testimony by: Gerald R. Patterson, Research Scientist—Oregon Social Learning Center, Eugene, Oregon; David Farrington, and John Monahan.

Ounces of Prevention: Toward an Understanding of the Causes of Violence; by State of California Commission on Crime Control and Violence Prevention, 1982.

DEMONSTRATING WITH HAND PUPPETS

Puppets appeal to all ages, children and adults alike, and afford an excellent means to act out the situations, emotions, and skills portrayed in the social skills lessons in this book. Moreover, a hand-crafted puppet is much better than one bought in a store. It is truly one of a kind.

The following pages present a variety of reproducible patterns for making hand and stick puppets for use with many of the lessons. The patterns can be photocopied just as they appear and used to make:

(1) Stationary Puppets: Color, cut out, glue onto cardboard, and tape onto a stick handle.

(2) Movable Puppets: Color, cut out, and glue onto felt shapes. Insert the hand inside the felt shapes so that the puppets can move.

Of course there are many varieties of hand puppets, each having a character and personality of its own, and equally suitable for demonstrating the situations and skills in the lessons. Examples include finger puppets, box puppets, paper bag puppets, glove and mitten puppets, and cylinder or tube puppets. Easy-to-follow, illustrated directions for making each of these types of puppets and others may be found in *Let's Discover Puppets* (West Nyack, NY: The Center for Applied Research in Education), by Jenean Romberg.

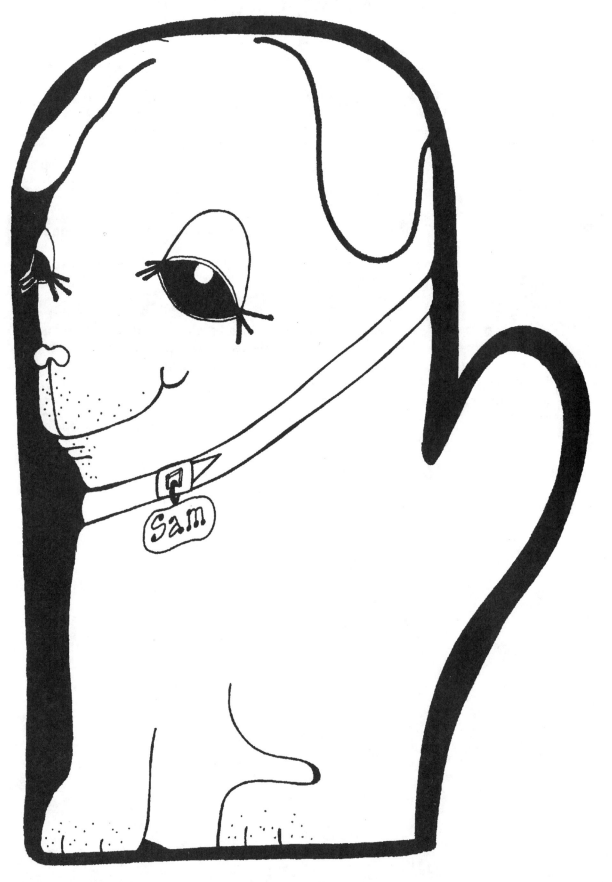

CONTENTS

      Reproducibles   "Sensitive Sam" Hand Puppet
                               "Social Sue" Hand Puppet
                               Morty Mouse Stick Puppet
                               Maggie Mouse Stick Puppet

SOCIAL SKILLS LESSONS & ACTIVITIES FOR GRADES 1–3

Lesson	*Social Skill*	*Page*

DISCIPLINARY STRATEGIES/CORRECTIVE ACTIONS

THINKING BEFORE ACTING

Contents

Contents

Contents

"PARTNERS IN SOCIAL SKILLS: A FAMILY AFFAIR"
(SINGLE PAGES REPRODUCIBLE AS MARKED)

Skill No. 1	Giving Compliments
Skill No. 2	Asking Permission
Skill No. 3	Disciplinary Strategies
Skill No. 4	Respect for Others
Skill No. 5	Using Self-Control
Skill No. 6	Improving Self-Image
Skill No. 7	Expressing Feelings
Skill No. 8	Accepting Consequences
Skill No. 9	Reacting to Failure
Skill No. 10	Setting Goals
Skill No. 11	Dealing with Prejudice
Skill No. 12	Dealing with Anger
Skill No. 13	Dealing with Peer Pressure
Skill No. 14	Problem Solving

Contents

SOCIAL SKILLS LESSONS & ACTIVITIES FOR GRADES 1-3

TO THE TEACHER

The following pages present 68 ready-to-use social skills lessons with a variety of related activities and worksheets. All of the lessons have been tested and are suggested for use with children in grades 1–3.

The lessons may be used in any order you desire, though they are sequenced in a general way, beginning with disciplinary strategies for the classroom. Ultimately, of course, you will match the needs and ability levels of your pupils with the particular lessons and social skills learning objectives. Some of the lessons may have to be repeated several times over the course of the school year.

You may wish to introduce a social skill in class discussion before presenting the related lesson, as suggested in the "Social Skills Task Review" on page 232. This should give you an idea of how familiar children may or may not be with the skill. The skill can then be discussed by the class again following the lesson to see how many children have learned the skill.

The patterns and worksheets accompanying these lessons may be photocopied as many times as you need them for use with individual children, small groups, or the whole class. You may also devise activity sheets of your own to enrich and reinforce any of the lessons.

SOCIAL SKILL
Accepting Disciplinary Actions

Behavioral Objective: The children will be able to recognize and accept disciplinary actions that are a consequence of their behavior.

Directed Lesson:

1. **Establish the Need:** The purpose is to enforce appropriate disciplinary action when necessary, by taking away or adding activities which the student enjoys.

2. **Introduction:** The teacher will ask the following questions and discuss the answers with the children.

    1. **Why do we need rules?**
    2. **How can we work together to follow our rules?**
    3. **Do we need disciplinary actions for rules that are broken? Why or why not?**

3. **Identify the Skill Components:** List the following skill components on the board or on sentence strips. Display classroom rules and consequences in the classroom, on a wall chart.

    1. Learn the class rules. Write them on a display chart.
    2. Learn the consequences for breaking those rules. Write them also on a display chart.

4. **Model the Skill:** The teacher tells the class that he/she is going to pretend to break one of the class rules. This will be his/her *first* time breaking a rule. The children will then choose the correct consequence. The teacher will pretend to break another rule, this time it will be her *second* time breaking a rule. Children again, will select the correct consequence. Discuss each rule and related consequence.

5. **Behavioral Rehearsal:**

    A. *Selection:* Teacher will select children to role play the breaking of a class rule.

    B. *Role Play:* Children will role play the breaking of 3 or 4 class rules. The class will then choose the appropriate consequence based on the rule broken, and the number of times that that particular rule was broken.

    C. *Completion:* After each role play, reinforce correct behavior. Identify inappropriate behavior, and reenact role play with corrections. If there are no corrections, role play is complete.

    D. *Reinforcers:* Progress charts with stars or stickers for children who have followed the rules. Stars, or stickers, or awards worn on clothes, foreheads or back of hands for all to see. Verbal praise (Example: "I like the way _____ followed our rules today").

1

E. *Discussion:* Discuss the correctness of the role play after each role play situation.

6. **Practice:** Hand out copies of the following activity sheet, "Happiness is Following Class Rules." Children will print the classroom rules and consequences on their papers.

7. **Independent Usage:** Give children copies of the family rules book activity sheet, "Happiness is Following Family Rules," to take home. Children will choose and write one of the rules used at home, and write the consequence if that rule is broken. Children may choose to draw a picture of that rule and the consequence if they wish.

8. **Continuation:** The teacher will tell the children that continued use of this social skill will bring about more happiness and harmony in their lives. The teacher should point out the need for this skill as related situations arise. There will be discussions about the children's home rules and consequences.

Name _____

Date _____

HAPPINESS IS FOLLOWING CLASS RULES

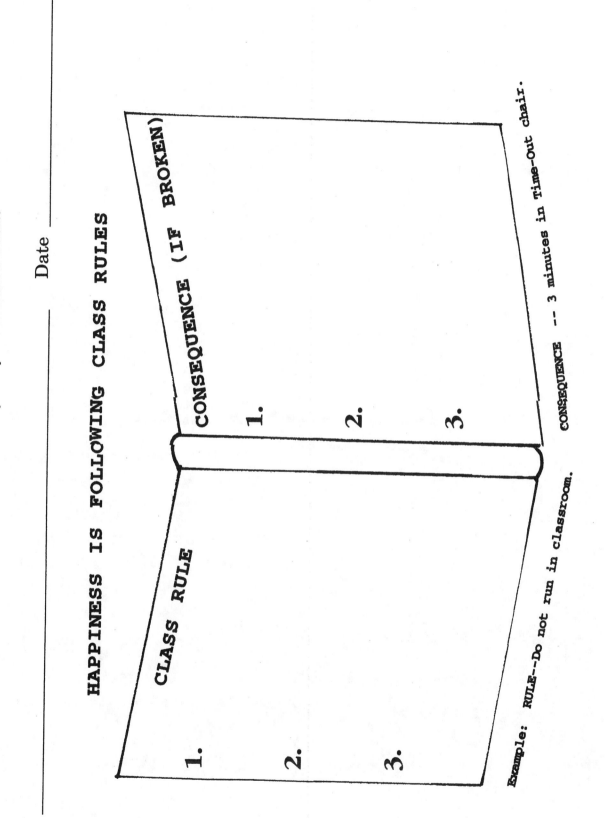

CLASS RULE

1.

2.

3.

CONSEQUENCE (IF BROKEN)

1.

2.

3.

Example: RULE--Do not run in classroom.   CONSEQUENCE -- 3 minutes in Time-Out chair.

Name _____

Date _____

HAPPINESS IS FOLLOWING FAMILY RULES

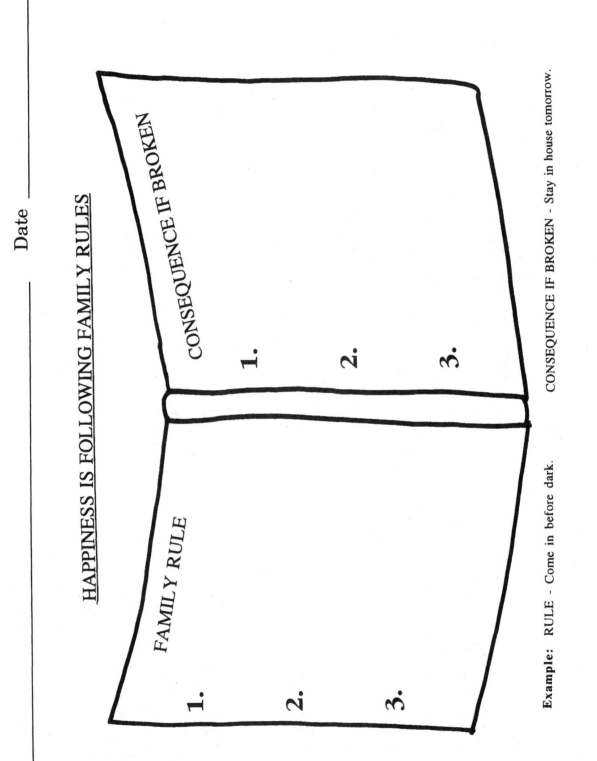

CONSEQUENCE IF BROKEN

1.

2.

3.

FAMILY RULE

1.

2.

3.

Example: RULE - Come in before dark.   CONSEQUENCE IF BROKEN - Stay in house tomorrow.

SOCIAL SKILL

Recognizing the Need for Disciplinary Actions

Behavioral Objective: The children will be able to recognize the need for disciplinary actions. These needs are: to avoid uncomfortable and negative behavior, ensure an environment inducive to learning, and living with others.

Directed Lesson:

1. **Establish the Need:** The teacher initiates a discussion about the relevance and benefits of the skill. Children need to be involved in the disciplinary process in order to accept and understand why discipline is necessary, when more than one person is involved.

2. **Introduction:** The teacher will say **"We are going to create a list of class rules and consequences."** Teacher establishes rules on the board or on sentence strips. Discuss why rules are important and the importance of the consequences to fit the broken rule.

3. **Identify the Skill Components:** Write the following skill components on the board or on sentence strips. Display rules and consequences in the classroom.

    1. Develop rules.
    2. Develop strategies.
    3. Develop consequences.
    4. Follow the rules.
    5. Accept the consequences, if rules are broken.

4. **Model the Skill:** The teacher will model the skill by using puppets. The puppets will portray a teacher and a problem animal. The teacher's puppet should demonstrate appropriate disciplinary action following the consequences set up by the class.

5. **Behavioral Rehearsal:**

    A. *Selection:* The teacher carefully selects one student to role play a teacher.

    B. *Role Play:* The teacher/student is in charge of the class. The teacher portrays a problem child. What happens when one person disrupts the entire class? What consequences should be followed according to the class rules?

    C. *Completion:* Following each role play, reinforce correct behavior, identify inappropriate behaviors and reenact role play with corrections. When role play is done correctly, it is complete.

    D. *Reinforcers:* Reinforce correct behavior with encouragement, group reinforcement, and non-verbal expressions of approval.

E. *Discussion:* Have the class discuss the role plays and the corrections that were made in each situation. Ask the class why it is necessary to have consequences for inappropriate behavior. What would happen if people were allowed to do anything they wished?

6. ***Practice:*** Give students copies of the following activity sheet, "Classroom Rules and Consequences," and have them copy the list of class rules and consequences to keep on file. They should sign their names showing responsibility for their actions and have parents sign the sheet.

7. ***Independent Use:***

   A. Students develop rules and consequences which could be applied in the lunchroom and on the playground.

   B. Students will develop rules and their consequences if broken. These rules and consequences could be applied at home using the worksheet entitled "Homework Rules and Consequences."

   C. Students will pledge to follow rules or to accept the consequences.

8. ***Continuation:*** Teacher should continue to point out the need to follow the rules.

CHILDREN'S LITERATURE

Greenfield, Eloise. *She Come Bringing Me That Little Baby Girl.* New York: Harper Collins Children's Books, 1993.

Walter, Mildred Pitts. *My Mama Needs Me.* New York: Lothrop, 1983.

Name_____   Date _____

CLASSROOM RULES AND CONSEQUENCES

I, the student, do hereby agree to follow the rules and to accept the consequences of my actions.

These are our Classroom Rules:

1.

2.

3.

4.

List Consequences (use student suggestions)

1.

2.

3.

_____   _____
(Parent Signature)   (Date)

Name _____   Date _____

HOMEWORK RULES AND CONSEQUENCES

These are the rules that I have set up with my parents so that I can get my homework done.

RULES:

1.

2.

3.

CONSEQUENCES: (This is what happens if I don't do the work).

1.

2.

3.

_____   _____
(Parent Signature)   (Date)

SOCIAL SKILL
Avoiding Negative Behavior

Behavioral Objective: The children will practice avoiding uncontrolled negative behavior to assure an environment conducive to learning and living productively.

Directed Lesson:

1. **Establish the Need:** Teacher initiates a discussion about the importance of the enforcement of rules. **"When rules are broken, there must be consequences. If there is no discipline, then people do whatever they want and nothing is accomplished."**

2. **Introduction:** Ask the students the following questions, and discuss their responses:

   "What would happen in our country if nothing were done to a person when they broke or disobeyed a rule? Would the country become a better place to live? Why?"

3. **Identify the Skill Components:** List the following skill components on the board or on sentence strips.

   1. Think about the behavior.
   2. Discuss possible consequences.
   3. Choose the most appropriate action.

4. **Model the Skill:** Teacher uses a list of established school/classroom rules visible in the room. (*Note:* Rules should be developed in a positive manner). Have the students look at Rule #1. Go through the skill steps by first asking them to think about the behavior. Ask for possible consequences if the rule is broken. (List suggestions on the board.) Ask them to choose the most appropriate consequence.

5. **Behavioral Rehearsal:**

   A. *Selection:* Teacher selects various students.
   B. *Role Play:* One student should be chosen to act as the teacher, and three others chosen to act as students. Teacher to students: Class look at the second rule. John would you read it please? Sally, what should we do first? Sally: Think about the behavior. Teacher: Good! What are some possible consequences? John. Sally. What is the most appropriate action? Bill?

   Role Play: One student acts as teacher and reads the skill steps. The other students will read the rules and discuss the steps to obtain an appropriate disciplinary action.

9

    C. *Completion:* After each role play, reinforce correct behavior, identify inappropriate behaviors, and reenact role play with corrections. If there are no corrections, role play is complete.

    D. *Reinforcers:* Use verbal praise or a smile and nod to show approval.

    E. *Discussion:* Have students discuss role plays and corrections made. Ask the class why it is important to be able to choose appropriate consequences for one's behavior.

6.   **Practice:** Hand out copies of the following activity sheet entitled "Classroom Rules and Consequences" and have students copy the lists of classroom rules and consequences. Next, divide class into groups. Assign Group A to make a poster of rules, and Group B to make a poster of consequences.

7.   **Independent Use:** Give students copies of the activity sheet entitled "Every Home Needs Rules" to decorate and color, then take home and complete. Place where it can be seen.

8.   **Continuation:** Teacher should remind students of the need for this skill as related situations occur.

CHILDREN'S LITERATURE

Aardema, Verna. *Why Mosquitos Buzz in People's Ears: A West African Tale.* New York: Puffin Books, 1993.

Rosen, Michael. *How the Animals Got Their Colors.*

Name_____   Date _____

CLASSROOM RULES AND CONSEQUENCES

Divide the class into two groups. Call one GROUP A and one GROUP B. Each group has a job to do!

GROUP A. *Make a BIG poster of your classroom rules. Use the space below for planning.*

GROUP B. *Make a BIG poster of the Consequences. Use the space below for planning.*

Name_____   Date _____

EVERY HOME NEEDS RULES

This is my refrigerator page. After I decorate it, I will take it home and use magnets to hold it onto the refrigerator door for all to see. Our family can work on the rules together.

HOME RULES:

1.

2.

3.

4.

THIS IS THE "OOPS!" PART. IF THE RULES ARE NOT FOLLOWED, WE AGREE THAT THESE ARE THE CONSEQUENCES:

1.

2.

3.

SOCIAL SKILL
Finding All Facts Before Acting

Behavioral Objective: The children will learn to think of all the reasons responsible for creating a given situation or conflict before taking action.

Directed Lesson:

1. ***Establish the Need:*** The purpose is to understand reasons, both physical and psychological conditions of the person and to also understand the problem so as to not attack the person, but the problem.

2. ***Introduction:*** The teacher will read the following story to the class:

   "Mrs. Jones looked up from her reading group one day to see Mandy crying. Mrs. Jones asked Mandy what was wrong. Mandy said that Jim had broken her red crayon. The teacher then asked Jim if he broke Mandy's red crayon. Jim said yes, but Mandy had taken his red crayon and thrown it away. 'Mandy, did you throw Jim's crayon away?' Mandy said she had seen it on the floor in front of the door, and was afraid someone would step on it and fall. She didn't know whose crayon it was and she didn't want to interrupt the class to find out, so she threw it away."

   Teacher asks class: **"Did Jim know the total situation before reacting?"** (Discussion follows.)

3. ***Identify the Skill Components:*** Write the following skill components on the board or on sentence strips before class.

   1. Gather all facts first.
   2. Think about all facts.
   3. Take appropriate action.

4. ***Model the Skill:*** Teacher demonstrates gathering all information about a situation before taking action.

   Example: The teacher is busy with a reading group, and sees Russ leave the room. Should she/he scold Russ for leaving without permission? No, she/he should go to the door to investigate. At the door is Russ's mom who brought a cake as a birthday surprise.

5. ***Behavioral Rehearsal:***

   A. *Selection:* The teacher asks for volunteers or selects students to role play.

B. *Role Play:* The students play the role of Mrs. Jones, Mandy and Jim from the Introduction and/or the teacher, Russ, and Russ's mom from the example in Modeling the Skill. (Other situations familiar to the group may be used, and children may suggest solutions such as having a lost and found box for items on the floor.)

C. *Completion:* After each role play, reinforce correct behavior, identify inappropriate behaviors, and reenact role play with corrections. If there are no corrections, role play is complete.

D. *Reinforcers:* During the role plays, the teacher will use verbal rewards and expressions of praise to provide reinforcement. Praise and appreciation should be used often throughout the school year to maintain the skill.

E. *Discussion:* The teacher can discuss and reinforce the positive outcomes from understanding *all* information before taking action. What observations did the class make?

6. **Practice:** Hand out copies of the following activity sheet entitled *The Sentence Egg Basket* and explain it to students. Have them color the eggs and basket then cut out the eggs and arrange them on the basket to say:

Gather All Facts First

7. **Independent Use:** Distribute copies of the activity sheet entitled "Be a Good Detective!" Have children discuss this social skill at home and color the picture. Parent is to sign activity sheet and make comments.

8. **Continuation:** The teacher reminds the class of the importance of finding *all* facts before acting. This will help in both social and academic relationships. Maintaining this skill is an ongoing process. Teacher should bring this to students attention as behaviors occur throughout the year.

CHILDREN'S LITERATURE

DePaola, Tomie. *Strega Nona.* New York: Simon & Schuster, 1979.

Duvoisin, Roger. *Petunia.* New York: Knopf Books for Young Readers, 1962.

Name_____   Date _____

THE SENTENCE EGG BASKET

Directions: Make a sentence using the four words in the eggs. Put a number "1" in the square by the word that is first, and "2" in the next word square, and so on. Then read your sentence. Choose four colors to make the page look bright and cheerful.

Name _____ Date _____

BE A GOOD DETECTIVE!

Find ALL the facts BEFORE you act!

Parent Comments

_____
_____
_____

signature

SOCIAL SKILL

Fully Understanding a Situation Before Acting

Behavioral Objective: The children will learn to assess the total situation before taking action, so as not to make a mistake when deciding upon a course of action.

Directed Lesson:

1. ***Establish the Need:*** The teacher begins a discussion about the benefits and relevance of the skill. It is important to understand that how to act depends on the total knowledge of how the situation developed.

2. ***Introduction:*** The teacher will introduce the skill by telling the following story:

    "Two children are playing ball in the street. Their ball accidentally breaks a window. The children run to the window to check the damage. They knock at the door, but no one answers. They remember the owner returns from work about 5:00 P.M. One child suggests trying to raise the money to fix the window before the owner returns. The children then run off.

    "The owner of the house returns early. He sees the broken window and calls the police. The police arrive just as the children return with the money. The owner angrily points at the children as they approach."

    The teacher discusses the story with the class. How does the owner feel? What do the police think? What do the children think and feel? The discussion should emphasize the gathering of knowledge of the whole situation before taking action.

3. ***Identify the Skill Components:*** Write the following skill components on the board or sentence strips.

    1. Ask/tell what happened.
    2. Ask questions.
    3. Listen to answers.
    4. Make decisions.

4. ***Model the Skill:*** The teacher walks into the classroom to find a box of pencils spilled on the floor. One child is busy picking them up, another is sitting at a desk. The teacher asks questions to determine what happened. Did the child picking up the pencils knock them over or is the child just covering up for another student?

5. ***Behavioral Rehearsal:***

    A. *Selection:* Teacher selects five children to role play.

B. *Role Play:* Two children begin to play catch in a street. One child throws the ball, hits and breaks a window. They discuss raising the money for the window before the owner returns. They leave to get the money.

C. *Completion:* Following each role play, reinforce correct behavior, identify inappropriate behaviors and re-enact role play with corrections. When role play is done correctly, it is complete.

D. *Reinforcers:* Acknowledge correct behavior with verbal encouragement, group reinforcement and non-verbal expressions of approval.

E. *Discussion:* Have the children discuss the merits of investigating the situation before taking action. Encourage them to talk about experiences they have encountered where someone was wrongly accused.

6. *Practice:* Hand out copies of the activity sheet entitled "What Happened Next?" for children to complete. They are to examine the pictures and write what happened in each case.

7. *Independent Use:*

A. Students will write a sentence explaining a situation then illustrate it, using the activity sheet "But, I Didn't Do It!"

B. Students will relate a situation which occurred at home.

C. Students will exhibit appropriate behavior in school situations.

8. *Continuation:* Teachers should continue pointing out the need to listen carefully before making decisions on how to act.

CHILDREN'S LITERATURE

Barracca, Debra and Sal. *Maxi, The Star.* New York: Dial Books for Young Readers, 1993.

Name _____   Date _____

WHAT HAPPENED NEXT?

Look at the pictures. Write what could happen next.

A. _____

_____

_____

_____

_____

B. _____

_____

_____

_____

_____

C. _____

_____

_____

_____

_____

Name_____ Date _____

"BUT, I DIDN'T DO IT!"

Directions: Write a complete sentence about something for which you were blamed, but did not do.

_____

_____

_____

_____

Draw a picture to help you tell your story.

HOW DID IT END?

SOCIAL SKILL

Assessing the Total Situation Before Acting

Behavioral Objective: The children will be able to assess the total situation before taking action.

Directed Lesson:

1. ***Establish the Need:*** Teacher discusses with the class the importance of assessing a situation before taking action. **"When a person understands the situation, they can then decide on what action to take. By doing this, they can possibly keep from making the wrong decision or from feeling bad about the decision they made."**

2. ***Introduction:*** Teacher tells the following story to the class:

    "Johnny couldn't find his crayons. He remembered loaning them to Paul. Since Paul didn't give them back, he went up to the teacher, and accused Paul of taking them, but Paul didn't have the crayons." Teacher then asks the following questions: **"What should Johnny have done before accusing Paul? If he had done these things first, then what might have happened?"** Lead class to the conclusion of looking at the total situation before acting. How would you feel if you accused someone only to find out later that you were wrong?

3. ***Identify the Skill Components:*** Write the following skill components on the board or place them on sentence strips.

    1. Investigate the situation in its completeness.
    2. Look at possible things that might have happened.
    3. Decide on what action to take.
    4. Do it.

4. ***Model the Skill:*** Teacher reads the following situation: **"The class was lining up to go to the lavatory. Lamar bumped into Erik."** Teacher then goes through skill steps to show how the problem was solved.

5. ***Behavioral Rehearsal:***

    A. *Selection:* One student is selected to read the setting. Two other students are used for the dialog.

    B. *Role Play:* (Place the parts on index cards.)

Setting: Class leaves the room, and Terry is the last one to leave because he was putting something in his desk. When class returns, it's just about lunchtime.

Dialogue Parts:

Sue:	"Teacher, someone stole my lunch."
Teacher:	"Let's think of what possibly could have happened to your lunch."
Sue:	"Terry took it!"
Teacher:	"You don't know that. Did you look in your desk?"
Tommy:	"Did you leave it on the bus?"
Ann:	"Maybe someone came into the room and took it."
Teacher:	"Sue, look again in the coatroom. And don't forget to check the back cupboard where you went to place your lunch envelope for milk."
Sue:	"All right, I'll look again. Gee! Here it is on the back cupboard."

C. *Completion:* After the role play, reinforce correct behavior, and identify inappropriate behavior. Reenact role play with corrections. If there are no corrections, role play is complete.

D. *Reinforcers:* Correct behavior should be reinforced by verbal praise, self-praise, and group encouragement.

E. *Discussion:* Students will discuss other occasions where understanding the total situation is necessary before taking action. Also, focus upon the result after taking action.

6. **Practice:** Hand out copies of the activity sheet entitled "The Missing Lunch Money." Do this together in class and discuss the actions taken.

7. **Independent Usage:** Distribute copies of the activity sheet "Family Viewpoint" for students to take home and complete. Ask them to bring the activity back for sharing and discussion.

8. **Continuation:** Teacher should remind children of the need to check all facts before taking action.

CHILDREN'S LITERATURE

Keats, Ezra Jack. *Goggles!* New York: Macmillan Children's Group (Aladdin), 1987.

Name_____   Date _____

THE MISSING LUNCH MONEY

The cat thinks the mouse has taken his lunch money. But did the mouse do it? Did the cat look in his desk? Did he look in his coat pocket? Where could it be, oh my oh me!

Write your story below.

Name_____ Date _____

FAMILY VIEWPOINT

Ask members of your family to think of situations when they failed to look at the total situation before taking action. Be prepared to share these situations with the class.

_____

_____

_____

_____

_____

_____

_____

_____

_____

_____

_____

_____

_____

_____

SOCIAL SKILL
Listening Attentively

Behavioral Objective: The learner will listen attentively when the teacher or another person is speaking to the class.

Directed Lesson:

1. ***Establish the Need:*** Teacher initiates a discussion about the relevance and benefits of the skill. Listening is needed in following directions and completing work.

2. ***Introduction:*** For practice, the teacher will say a sentence. The student will repeat that sentence and add a rhyming sentence.

   Example: (teacher) There once was a cat, who ran after a _____.

            (student) There once was a cat, who ran after a bat.

   Next, the teacher will ask the students to listen to the poem and think of words that rhyme with *an.*

   > **"I knew a man,**
   > **His name was ____an.**
   > **He fried eggs in a ____an.**
   > **He cooled off by the ____an.**
   > **He drove a ____an.**
   > **The color was ____an.**
   > **When his friends asked if he could sing,**
   > **He said, 'Yes, I ____an.'"**

3. ***Identify the Skill Components:*** List the following skill components on the board before class.

   1. Look at the speaker.
   2. Sit quietly.
   3. Think about what the speaker said.
   4. Answer the question.

4. ***Model the Skill:*** Teacher will play the role of the student and teacher. As teacher, she will read aloud from a book, and ask a question. As student, she will answer the question.

5. ***Behavorial Rehearsal:***

   A. *Selection:* Teacher selects five students to play the following roles: one teacher and four students. Teacher will give the role playing teacher question cards to read individually to the four students.

25

B. *Role Play:* Activity cards can be adapted to fit the needs and level of the children.

C. *Completion:* After each role play, reinforce correct behavior, identify inappropriate behaviors, and reenact role play with corrections. If there are no corrections, role play is complete.

D. *Reinforcers:* Correct behavior should be acknowledged by verbal praise, non-verbal expressions of approval and self-praise (pat yourself on the back if you guessed some of the answers to the poem and role plays). Have a big garden glove available that students can use to pat themselves on the back.

E. *Discussion:* Have children discuss the role plays and the corrections that were made. Ask the class what advantages there are in listening to a speaker. Are there any disadvantages? Discuss what problems they have with the skill.

6. *Practice:* Hand out copies of the following "Draw the Answer" activity sheet. Children will answer questions 1,2,3, and 4 then color the pictures in class.

7. *Independent Use:* Ask students to watch the evening news. The following morning the students will be asked to tell what they listened to on the news.

8. *Continuation:* Teachers should remind children of the importance of listening attentively as related situations arise.

CHILDREN'S LITERATURE

Dr. Seuss. *The Cat in the Hat.* New York: Random House Books for Young Readers, 1966.

Johson, Angela. *Tell Me a Story, Mama.* New York: Orchard Books Watts, 1989.

Name _____   Date _____

DRAW THE ANSWER

---

①   1.   **Three apples <u>and</u> three apples equals _____ apples.**

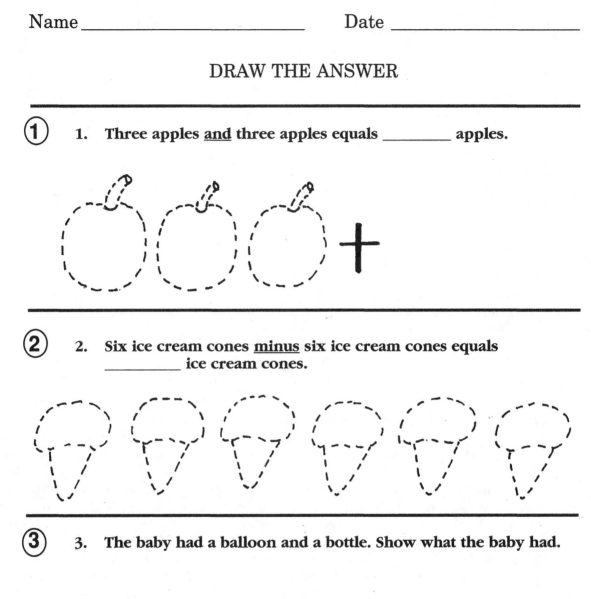

---

②   2.   **Six ice cream cones <u>minus</u> six ice cream cones equals _____ ice cream cones.**

---

③   3.   **The baby had a balloon and a bottle. Show what the baby had.**

---

④   4.   **The house has four windows and one door. Show what the house has.**

© 1995 by Society for Prevention of Violence

SOCIAL SKILL

Listening (for Prediction)

Behavorial Objective: The children will listen attentively when the teacher or another person is speaking to the class.

Directed Lesson:

1. **Establish the Need:** The teacher initiates a discussion about the relevance of the skill. Listening is an extremely important skill to master. It is the basis for all learning. Without good listening skills, children will not be able to follow directions or understand their work. This skill is necessary for any learning to take place.

2. **Introduction:** The teacher will introduce the skill by reading the following story to the class. Tell the students to be prepared to answer and ask questions about the story.

   "Long ago in the land of _____ (school) there lived a little girl by the name of Lisette. She was very unhappy because she never knew what was going on. One day, she hopped onto her pet dragon, Cyril, and began a journey to discover the solution to her problem. Lisette flew to her teacher's house and asked 'Mrs. Apple, why is it so hard for me to learn in school?' As Mrs. Apple began to answer her, Lisette turned her head to listen to a bird singing in a tree. When she turned around, Mrs. Apple had finished her explanation. Lisette still didn't have an answer. She hopped back on Cyril and flew to her friend, Harry's house. She asked Harry the same question. As he began to reply, Lisette turned her head to watch Cyril and Harry's dragon play together. When she turned around, Harry had finished his explanation. Lisette still didn't have an answer. She hopped back on Cyril, but he refused to move. Cyril said to her, 'Lisette, the reason you have trouble learning in school and the reason you never know what is going on around you is....'"

   Teacher: **"Children, what do you think Cyril is going to say?"**

   Correct: **"Yes, it is because you never listen to the person who is speaking."**

   The teacher may have children answer or ask questions about the story to check listening levels.

3. **Identify the Skill Components:** List the following skill components on the board before class.

   1. Look at the person who is speaking.

   2. Sit quietly while the person is talking.

   3. Think about what is being said.

4. Answer questions.

5. Ask questions.

4. ***Model the Skill:*** The teacher models the skill steps by listening to a child reading from a book and answering any questions from the class.

5. ***Behavioral Rehearsal:***

   A. *Selection:* The teacher selects four pairs of children to role play. They may be volunteers or children that the teacher feels need the practice.

   B. *Role Play:* The pairs of children will act out the following:
      1. Child reads, another child listens.
      2. Child tells about T.V. show, another child listens.
      3. Child pretends to be parent talking to child, the other child listens.
      4. Child pretends to be teacher explaining a math problem, the other child listens.

   C. *Completion:* After each role play, reinforce correct behavior, identify inappropriate behaviors, and reenact role play with corrections. If there are no corrections, role play is complete.

   D. *Reinforcers:* Reinforce appropriate behaviors with verbal encouragement, tangible rewards, and physical displays of approval (i.e., hug, pat, smile).

   E. *Discussion:* Have children discuss the various role plays, the appropriate and inappropriate behaviors. Ask them to formulate their own conclusions as to the importance of listening. What problems do they have trying to listen?

6. ***Practice:*** Distribute copies of the activity sheet "Listen for the Color." The children will listen for the color of the animals in the following poem, then write the colors and color in the animals.

   POEM: (Read it slowly to the class. Reread and give time to write colors.)

   "There once was a *pig* whose color was *red*
   And all he wanted was to be fed.
   He had a good friend who was a *goat*
   The goat was *green* from his toes to his throat.
   And then there was Charlie, an active *dog*,
   He turned *purple* when he started to jog.
   Of course we know the *kitten* of *yellow*
   He was such a funny fellow!
   The *horse* walked right into the sea
   To get *blue* water on each knee.
   And now we'll finish with the sleepy *owl*
   Whose *brownish* color came off on his towel!"

7. ***Independent Use:*** Encourage the family to use the public library and to read or tell a story to the child. Ask the child to answer or ask questions about the story, and to share the experience with the group.

8.   ***Continuation:*** The teacher should continually point out to children that good listening is necessary for learning.

CHILDREN'S LITERATURE

Paterson, Katherine. *The Tale of the Mandarin Ducks.* New York: Dutton Children's Books, 1990.

Name _____ Date _____

LISTEN FOR THE COLOR

Directions: The teacher will read a poem aloud. Listen carefully for the color of each animal. Write the color word for each animal on the line and then color the animal with that color.

pig _____   goat _____

dog _____   cat _____

horse _____   owl _____

SOCIAL SKILL
Listening for Specific Information

Behavioral Objective: The children will listen attentively when the teacher or another person is speaking to the class.

Directed Lesson:

1. **Establish the Need:** The teacher reviews with the class the importance of listening and what happens if students are not listening. Stress that no learning can take place unless there is active listening. . . hearing and understanding what is being said.

2. **Introduction:** Introduce the skills by means of a game. The teacher begins the game by starting a story and suddenly stopping. The teacher then calls on a volunteer in the class to continue the story, making sure that it relates to the previous information.

3. **Identify the Skill Components:** List the following skill components on the board before class.

   1. Look at the person who is speaking.
   2. Sit quietly while the person is talking.
   3. Think about what is being said.
   4. Answer questions.
   5. Ask questions.

4. **Model the Skill:** The teacher models the skill steps by listening to a child describe an item in the classroom.

5. **Behavioral Rehearsal:**

   A. *Selection:* Teacher selects ten children to role play.

   B. *Role Play:* Each child selects an animal, a food, or a means of transportation to describe to the class. The children must listen and figure out what is being described.

   C. *Completion:* After each role play, reinforce correct behavior, identify inappropriate behaviors, and reenact role play with corrections. If there are no corrections, role play is complete.

   D. *Reinforcers:* Compliment each child who has correctly answered and distribute "good listener" badges.

   E. *Discussion:* Discuss what advantages there are in listening to a speaker. What disadvantages are there in not listening to a speaker?

6. ***Practice:*** Distribute copies of the following activity sheet entitled *Listening* to the children.

    The teacher reads the following short description to the class. The children must answer questions relating to the information. The teacher will read it again stressing how important it is to listen in order to get information. The class then does the activity sheet together.

    Story: **"One Monday morning, three blue ducks decided to go to town. The ducks waited for a huge bus driven by a man with a funny hat."**

7. ***Independent Use:*** Children will listen to sounds they heard at home and write them down. There should be a minimum of five sounds. Also write down the time of day that the sounds were heard. Bring the list back to school. Collect them in a container and read them aloud.

8. ***Continuation:*** Teachers should point out the importance of listening carefully to get the correct information as related situations arise.

CHILDREN'S LITERATURE
(Animal Stories)

McClosky, Robert. *Make Way for Ducklings.* New York: Viking Children's Books, 1941.

Tafuri, Nancy. *Have You Seen My Duckling?* New York: Viking Children's Books, 1986.

Name _____   Date _____

LISTENING

After your teacher reads
you the story about ducks
fill in the blanks below.

1. What day of the week was it? _____

2. How many ducks were there? _____

3. What color were the ducks? _____

4. Where did the ducks want to go? _____

5. What did they ride in? _____

6. How big was it? _____

7. Who drove it? _____

8. What was he wearing? _____

SOCIAL SKILL
Listening for the Main Idea of a Story

Behavioral Objective: The children will state the main idea of the selection read by the teacher.

Directed Lesson:

1. **Establish the Need:** Teacher relates the qualities of a good listener: (A) one should look at the person speaking, and (B) be ready to repeat what the speaker said. What are some things that might happen if we don't listen?

2. **Introduction:** Teacher will read a short selection from the basal reader, and call upon children to identify the main idea of the selection.

3. **Identify the Skill Components:** List the following skill components on the board before class.

    1. Listen to a selection read from the basal reader.
    2. Verbally identify the main idea of the selection.

4. **Model the Skill:** Teacher will select a student to read a specific paragraph from the basal reader. Teacher will listen and state the main idea.

5. **Behavioral Rehearsal:**

    A. *Selection:* Teacher will divide the class into two teams, all students will participate in role play.

    B. *Role Play:* Teacher will read a paragraph and call on a team member to give the main idea. If the answer is correct, that student may select the listener for the other team. If the answer is incorrect, the other team may give their answer. Continue as time permits.

    C. *Completion:* After each role play, reinforce correct behavior, identify inappropriate behaviors, and reenact role play with corrections. If there are no corrections, role play is complete.

    D. *Reinforcers:* Give verbal encouragement, a nod of approval and smile, or certificates for correct behavior.

    E. *Discussion:* Students will make suggestions to improve role play.

6. **Practice:** Distribute copies of the following activity sheet, "Listening Ears," for children's completion in class.

7. ***Independent Use:***

   A. Students may practice the same role-play game in small groups during recess.

   B. Teacher will praise children who practice the qualities of being a good listener when someone else is speaking.

   C. Ask a family member to read a story, and have the child give the main idea.

8. ***Continuation:*** Teachers should remind children of the importance of listening for the main idea when someone is reading/speaking to them as related situations occur throughout the year.

CHILDREN'S LITERATURE

Ehlert, Lois. *Moon Rope: Un Lazo a la Luna.* San Diego: Harcourt Brace, 1992.

Isadora, Rachel. *Max.* New York: Macmillan Children's Group (Aladdin), 1984.

Name_____ Date _____

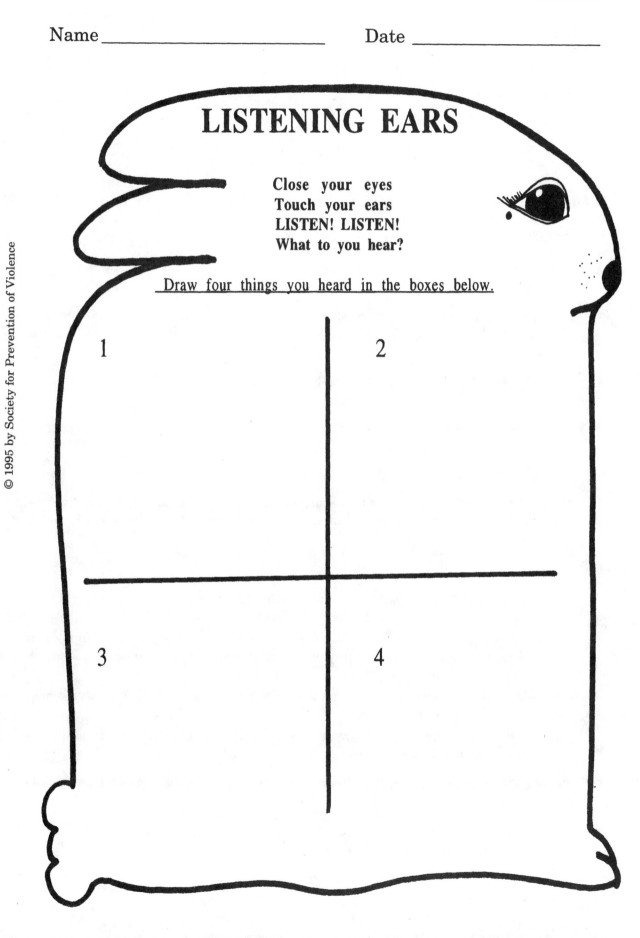

LISTENING EARS

Close your eyes
Touch your ears
LISTEN! LISTEN!
What to you hear?

Draw four things you heard in the boxes below.

1

2

3

4

SOCIAL SKILL
Listening for Details (Writing)

Behavioral Objective: Children will write a sentence dictated by the teacher.

Directed Lesson:

1. **Establish the Need:** Recap the qualities of a good listener and the advantages of being a good listener.

2. **Introduction:** Teacher tells children about a girl who won a $10.00 prize in a contest for remembering the most details and sequence of a story. The story was read aloud by the librarian.

3. **Identify the Skill Components:** (List on board before class)

    1. Listen and learn.
    2. Think about what has been said.
    3. Write a short sentence about what you learned.
    4. Read the sentence.

4. **Model the Skill:** The teacher dictates a sentence using words from the weekly spelling unit. The student will write the sentence. *Example:* "Vacation. We will go on *vacation* in June."

5. **Behavioral Rehearsal:**

    A. *Selection:* The whole class will write dictated sentences.

    B. *Role Play:* Children will listen to the teacher read the sentence once and will write it. Teacher will ask several students to read the sentence.

    C. *Completion:* After each role play, reinforce correct behavior, identify inappropriate behaviors, and reenact role play with corrections. If there are no corrections, role play is complete.

    D. *Reinforcers:* Give verbal praise and/or a star to those children who have correct answers.

    E. *Discussion:* Children will share their experiences with listening and carrying out the role play. Encourage them to suggest improvements.

6. **Practice:** Distribute copies of the activity sheet "Sentence Dictation" for children to complete in class.

7. **Independent Use:** Teams or individual children report progress to the teacher and earn a star to be put on a "Listening for Every Detail Chart."

8.   ***Continuation:*** Teachers should continue to point out the need for taking accurate dictation as related situations arise.

CHILDREN'S LITERATURE

DePaola, Tomie. *Fin M'Coul, the Giant of Knockmany Hill.* New York: Holiday, 1981.

Lobel, Anita. *Allison's Zinnia.* New York: Wm. Morrow (Greenwillow), 1990.

Name _____   Date _____

SENTENCE DICTATION

Directions: Select a friend to dictate four sentences to you from your favorite book. Write them below, and check them.

1. _____

   _____

2. _____

   _____

3. _____

   _____

4. _____

   _____

FOLLOWING DIRECTIONS

SOCIAL SKILL

Following Verbal Instructions

Behavioral Objective: The children will be able to follow the directions given by the teacher or another adult to the instructor's satisfaction.

Directed Lesson:

1. **Establish the Need:** Teacher initiates a discussion about the relevance and benefits of the skill. Following instructions by listening attentively enables the student to successfully complete tasks given by the teacher.

2. **Introduction:** Teacher will initiate a game of Simon Says. Teacher will explain (review) the rules of the game to the class. She will stress the importance of following the rules and commands of the game in order to remain in the game.

3. **Identify the Skill Components:** (List on board before class)

   1. Look at the speaker.
   2. Listen.
   3. Think about what the speaker is saying.
   4. Ask questions.
   5. Follow instructions.

4. **Model the Skill:** Teacher will read aloud the following instructions for making a "walkie-talkie," and will carry out the instructions.

   Materials: two paper cups; yarn; pencil; tape

   Directions:

   1. Using a pencil, poke a hole into the bottom of each paper cup.
   2. Slip the yarn through the inside of the hole in Cup #1 and tie a knot.
   3. Slip the yarn through the inside of the hole in Cup #2 and tie a knot.
   4. Place a piece of tape over each knot to hold it in place.
   5. Move the cups away from each other until yarn is taut.
   6. Teacher demonstrates how a "walkie-talkie" requires a speaker (sender) and a listener (receiver).

41

5. ***Behavioral Rehearsal:***

    A. *Selection:* Teacher selects three pairs of students to role play. In each pair, one person gives instructions while the other person completes the task.

    B. *Role Play:*

        1. One person tells the other person how to put on a coat.

        2. One person tells the other person how to sharpen a pencil at the pencil sharpener.

        3. One person tells the other person how to do a simple math problem on the board.

    C. *Completion:* After each role play, reinforce correct behavior, identify inappropriate behaviors, and reenact role play with corrections. If there are no corrections, role play is complete.

    D. *Reinforcers:* Praise correct behavior verbally and nonverbally, through a nod or a pat on the back.

    E. *Discussion:* After the role play, ask such questions as, "What did you have to do to stay in the game?" "What was the reason you had to sit down?" "Is it important to follow directions in school?" "Why?"

6. ***Practice:*** Teacher will read the instructions for any project and ask children to follow them.

    Distribute copies of the following "Walkie-Talkie" activity sheet for children to color, and encourage them to use their "walkie-talkie" sets during recess.

7. ***Independent Use:*** Set up a "Listening Center" in the classroom with recorder, head sets and story records or tapes. Children can go there in their spare time, or during indoor recess, to listen for pleasure and understanding.

8. ***Continuation:*** Teachers should continue to remind children that they are more likely to be successful in completing tasks given by the teacher if they follow his/her directions carefully.

CHILDREN'S LITERATURE
(Pleasure and Understanding)

Baer, Edith. *This Is the Way We Go to School.* New York: Scholastic, 1990.

Fox, Mem. *Possum Magic.* San Diego: Harcourt Brace, 1990.

Name _____   Date _____

WALKIE TALKIE

To make your own Walkie Talkie you will need two cups, string, and tape. FIRST, poke a tiny hole in the bottom of each cup. NEXT, pull the string through and tape it to the inside of the cup.

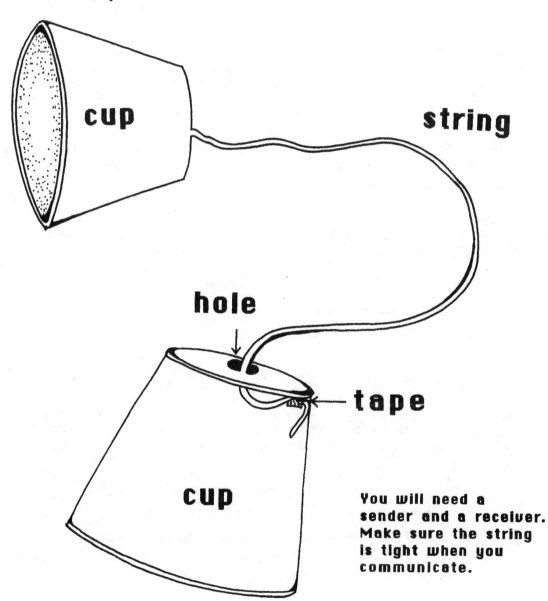

cup

string

hole

tape

cup

You will need a sender and a receiver. Make sure the string is tight when you communicate.

SOCIAL SKILL

Following Instructions for Safety

Behavioral Objective: The children will follow verbal instructions given by the teacher, or another adult, to the instructor's satisfaction.

Directed Lesson:

1. **Establish the Need:** Teacher begins a discussion about the benefits and relevance of the skill. Following instructions is a skill that students will use throughout their lives. In school, students who do not or cannot follow instructions will not remain on the task, will not complete assignments, and as a result, will likely disrupt other students. This will interfere with learning.

2. **Introduction:** The teacher will introduce the skill by saying, **"Sometimes you will be given instructions that could save your life if followed correctly or successfully. For example, if our building catches on fire, the fire alarm will sound to warn us to leave the building. It is *very* important that we follow our instructions for getting out of the building quickly, orderly, and safely. When the fire alarm sounds, we will quickly line up and walk out of the building. If everyone follows the instructions successfully, everyone will get out of the building safely."**

3. *Identify the Skill Components:* **(List on board before class)**

   1. Look at the person talking.
   2. Listen to the instructions.
   3. Think about what is being said.
   4. Answer questions.
   5. Follow the oral instructions.

4. **Model the Skill:** Teacher gives specific instructions for lining up. Children then practice the line-up. Next, teacher gives specific instructions for leaving the room, leaving the building, and going quickly and quietly to their designated outdoor area. Children then practice the routine twice.

5. **Behavioral Rehearsal:**

   A. *Selection:* Teacher selects pairs of children for role play activities.
   B. *Role Play:* Have children role play situations such as: tying your shoe laces, using the phone (pushbutton), jumping rope, cleaning desks, walking up and down stairs.

C. *Completion:* After each role play, reinforce correct behavior, identify inappropriate behaviors, and reenact role play with corrections. If there are no corrections, role play is complete.

D. *Reinforcers:* Acknowledge correct behavior with material rewards, verbal praise, non-verbal expressions of approval (i.e., smile, pat, hug), and group reinforcement. Select students to tape a story for the Listening Center.

E. *Discussion:* Have the children discuss the merits of following instructions. Ask them to describe what difficulties they might have in listening and following instructions. Discuss what consequences they might have if they don't follow the instructions.

6. **Practice:** Distribute copies of the activity sheet "Grow a Flower" along with crayons or other markers, construction paper and paste. Children will follow instructions given by the teacher, presented on the next page, to complete the flower.

7. **Independent Use:**

A. Students follow instructions in the lunchroom.

B. Students follow instructions for bus safety.

C. Students follow instructions of the school crossing guards.

8. **Continuation:** Teachers should continue to point out the need for this skill in virtually every aspect of our lives, as related situations arise.

CHILDREN'S LITERATURE

Solotareff, Gregoire. *Never Trust an Ogre!* New York: Wm. Morrow (Greenwillow), 1988.

Young, Ed. *Lon Po Po: A Red Riding Hood Story from China.* New York: Putnam Pub. Group, 1989.

VERBAL INSTRUCTIONS FOR
FLOWER ACTIVITY SHEET

The following are TEACHER'S INSTRUCTIONS for completing, coloring and constructing the flower activity sheet presented on the next page.

Please read these directions slowly to the class. Allow time for each instruction to be completed. Children need activity sheet and construction paper.

1. Get your crayons (watercolors, markers, colored chalk, colored pencils, or whatever you are using) out on your desk.

2. Look at the flower.

3. Color the inside of the circle black or brown.

4. Color the petals of the flower yellow.

5. Color the stem and leaves green.

6. Carefully cut out the parts of the flower.

7. Paste the stem on the construction paper you have been given, but remember, you must leave room at the top of the stem for the flower. The leaves of the stem should point to the top of the page.

8. Paste your flower at the top of your stem.

9. Write your name on the back of your paper.

© 1995 by Society for Prevention of Violence

CHILDREN'S ACTIVITY SHEET

Name _____   Date _____

GROW A FLOWER

Directions: Follow the instructions given by the teacher so that you can complete this flower.

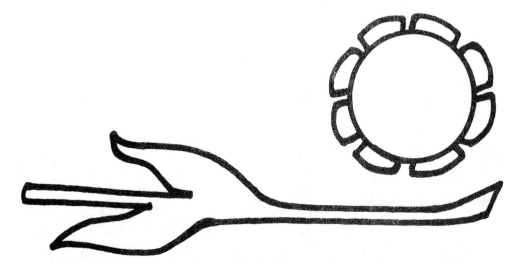

Name _____ Date _____

GROW A FLOWER

Directions: Follow the instructions given by the teacher so that you can complete this flower.

SOCIAL SKILL
Following Written Instructions

Behavioral Objective: The children will follow written instructions given by the teacher.

Directed Lesson:

1. **Establish the Need:** Teacher reviews the benefits and relevance of the skill. Following instructions is a skill that students will use throughout their lives. Students need to follow written directions in order to accomplish their school work. Not having this skill leads to failure.

2. **Introduction:** The teacher will introduce the skill by saying, **"Sometimes you will want to do something, or make something, or cook something, *and* you must follow the instructions exactly, if you want to be successful. You must learn to follow instructions carefully if you want to be successful in completing your school work."**

3. **Identify the Skill Components:** (List on board before class)

    1. Look at the instructions.
    2. Read the instructions.
    3. Think about what you read.
    4. Answer questions about the instructions if necessary.
    5. Follow the instructions.

4. **Model the Skill:** Teacher models the skill by reading and following the instructions posted for taking cover during a tornado warning.

5. **Behavioral Rehearsal:**

    A. *Selection:* Select ten children to role play the various activities.

    B. *Role Play:* Give students instructions (written) for completing classroom activities such as: how to put a heading on your paper; how to do an addition problem; or how to color a certain picture. The students will role play each activity. Use the chalkboard.

    C. *Completion:* After each role play, reinforce correct behavior, identify inappropriate behaviors, and reenact role play with corrections. If there are no corrections, role play is complete.

    D. *Reinforcers:* material rewards, verbal praise, non-verbal expressions of approval (i.e., smile, pat, hug), group reinforcement, being selected as leader of a class game.

E. *Discussion:* Have the children discuss the role plays and any inappropriate behaviors that needed correction. Discuss the difficulties of following written directions and how to overcome them. Relate this skill with activities outside of the classroom such as driving a car, going to school, following a recipe, etc.

6. ***Practice:*** Have students complete the following activity sheet, "Following Written Instructions." They must read and follow all the directions. There is a different direction for each line.

7. ***Independent Use:***

   1. Students read and follow directions to play a game.

   2. Students read and follow instructions for food preparation (lemonade).

   3. Students read and follow instructions to operate a simple appliance.

8. ***Continuation:*** Teachers should continue to remind children of the importance of following written directions carefully as related situations arise.

CHILDREN'S LITERATURE
(Following Directions)

Polacco, Patricia. *Thundercake.* New York: Putnam, 1990.

Name _____   Date _____

FOLLOWING WRITTEN INSTRUCTIONS

Directions: Follow all the directions written below.

1. Write your first name on line A.

2. Write your last name on line B.

3. Write the name of your school on line C.

4. Write the day of the week on line D.

5. Write your favorite color on line E.

6. Write the name of your best friend on line F.

7. Write the name of your favorite T.V. show on line G.

8. Write the name of your favorite T.V. actor on line H.

9. Write the name of your favorite food on line I.

10. Write the time that you are doing this worksheet on line J.

LINE A _____

LINE B _____

LINE C _____

LINE D _____

LINE E _____

LINE F _____

LINE G _____

LINE H _____

LINE I _____

LINE J _____

**FOLLOW
US
TO SUCCESS !!!**

SOCIAL SKILL
Following Verbal Directions at School

Behavioral Objective: The children will verbally repeat directions and carry them out.

Directed Lesson:

1. **Establish the Need:** Teacher stresses the importance of listening for directions. What might happen if we didn't have directions in case of a fire drill? A tornado drill? Teacher and students identify other instances where verbal directions are important. What would be some of the consequences of not following these directions?

2. **Introduction:** Teacher asks, **"What happens when we don't hear all of the directions?" "How are we rewarded for hearing all of the directions?" "What are the characteristics of a good listener?"**

3. **Identify the Skill Components:** (List on board before class)

   1. Listen to directions.
   2. Verbally repeat directions.
   3. Carry out the directions.

4. **Model the Skill:** The teacher will ask a student to give her/him instructions to write today's date on the chalkboard. Teacher will repeat directions and carry them out. Student will then give instructions to have teacher move a book in the room from Point A to Point B. Teacher will repeat the directions and carry them out.

5. **Behavioral Rehearsal:**

   A. *Selection:* Teacher will select eight pairs of students. One student will read directions and one will carry out directions, similar to those modeled above.

   B. *Role Play:* One student will read directions written on a card or board to a student. That student will repeat directions and carry them out. Repeat until all instructions are used. Instructions that are to be written on cards or board are as follows:

      1. Take your reading book out, and read page 10 aloud.
      2. Go put on your coat and stand by the window.
      3. Write your name and birthday on the chalkboard.
      4. Give the person next to you your math book.
      5. Give the teacher a book.
      6. Put the wastebasket under the flag.
      7. Wash your hands.
      8. Draw a yellow flower.

    C. *Completion:* After each role play, reinforce correct behavior, identify inappropriate behaviors, and reenact role play with corrections. If there are no corrections, role play is complete.

    D. *Reinforcers:*

       ▶ Verbal encouragement, such as "Super!," "Great!," etc.

       ▶ Physical nod of head to show approval, smile.

       ▶ Sit by a friend for the rest of the day.

    E. *Discussion:* Students will react to individual role plays and suggest improvement when necessary. Discuss benefits, consequences and difficulties of the skill.

6. **Practice:** Distribute copies of the following "Good Morning, Butterfly!" activity sheet for children to complete. Check their work to see how well they have followed the directions.

7. **Independent Use:**

    A. Teacher will encourage students to repeat directions quietly during the day for practice.

    B. During recess the students can read directions to each other and repeat them, scoring points for directions repeated correctly.

    C. Look for types of directions on T.V., on road signs, and at home. Give class time to share this information.

8. **Continuation:** Teacher should continue to remind children of the importance of listening for and following verbal directions both in and out of school.

CHILDREN'S LITERATURE

Fox, Mem. *Wilfrid Gordon McDonald Partridge.* Brooklyn, NY: Kane-Miller Books, 1985.

Kaye, Marilyn. *The Real Tooth Fairy.* San Diego: Harcourt Brace, 1990.

Name _____   Date _____

"GOOD MORNING, BUTTERFLY!"

Color the butterfly yellow and black. UNDER the butterfly make some green grass and pink flowers. Draw an insect in the grass.

SOCIAL SKILL
Following Directions at Play

Behavioral Objective: The children will follow the teacher's directions.

Directed Lesson:

1. ***Establish the Need:*** Teacher stresses the importance of following directions. Teacher and students make a list of why it's important to follow directions. We need directions to bake a cake, find a park, play a game, or fly a plane, etc. What would happen if there were no directions? (We couldn't do any one of these activities.)

2. ***Introduction:*** Teacher will give a series of directions. For example:

    A. Take out your reading book. Open it to Page 75.

    B. Get a sheet of paper, and write your name and today's date on the paper.

    C. On your paper, write the first word on P. 75.

3. ***Identify the Skill Components:*** (List on board before class)

    1. Listen carefully to teacher.

    2. Repeat the discussion silently.

    3. Complete the task.

4. ***Model the Skill:*** Teacher models the skill steps by following directions listed on a class chart.

    A. Stand up.

    B. Sit down.

    C. Hop on one foot.

    D. Put hands on your shoulders, etc.

5. ***Behavioral Rehearsal:***

    A. *Selection:* Teacher selects three students to be the leaders. The leaders play a game, e.g., Simon Says.

    B. *Role Play:* Description:

    "Simon says stand up."
    "Simon says sit in your seat."
    "Simon says stand up again."
    "Simon says hop three times."

C. *Completion:* After each role play, reinforce correct behavior, identify inappropriate behaviors, and reenact role play with corrections. If there are no corrections, role play is complete.

D. *Reinforcers:* (Verbal)

1. "Good listening!"
2. "You were great!"
3. "You were a good listener!"
4. "That's a good job!"

E. *Discussion:* Students will respond to role plays and give suggestions for improving role plays. Review why it is important to follow directions. What happens if you don't?

6. **Practice:** Give children copies of the accompanying activity sheet, "Following Directions in Math," to complete in class.

7. **Independent Usage:** Children can relate what directions they had to follow that week (i.e., lunchroom, travel, or bus safety).

8. **Continuation:** Teachers should stress the importance of following directions continually, as related situations arise.

CHILDREN'S LITERATURE

Carle, Eric. *The Very Hungry Caterpillar.* New York: Putnam Publishing Group, 1986.

_____. *One, Two, Three to the Zoo.* New York: Putnam Publishing Group, 1990.

Name _____   Date _____

FOLLOWING DIRECTIONS IN **MATH**

Directions:

1. **Add the problems in Box 1.**

2. **Subtract the problems in Box 2.**

3. **Follow the signs (+ and –) in Box 3.**

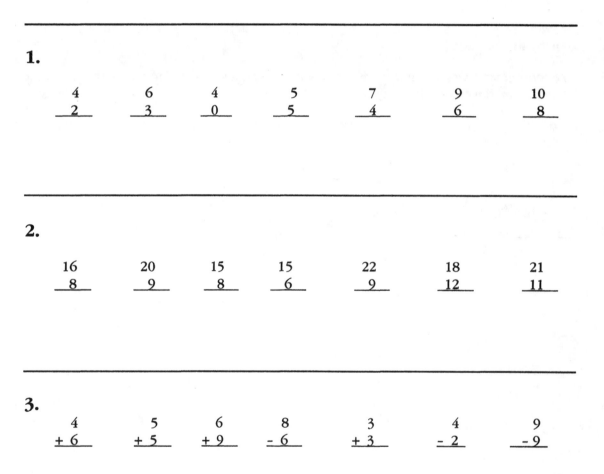

1.

4	6	4	5	7	9	10
2	3	0	5	4	6	8

2.

16	20	15	15	22	18	21
8	9	8	6	9	12	11

3.

4	5	6	8	3	4	9
+ 6	+ 5	+ 9	– 6	+ 3	– 2	– 9

SOCIAL SKILL
Feeling Good About Oneself

Behavioral Objective: The children will state something they like about themselves when asked.

Directed Lesson:

1. ***Establish the Need:*** Teacher initiates a discussion about the relevance and benefits of the behavior. Building a positive self-concept will help with success academically and socially.

2. ***Introduction:*** Teacher will use a puppet to recite the following riddle.

    Question: **Who Am I?**

    I know that I'm terrific,
    But let me be specific!
    I can run and play and move and walk
    I can drink and eat and sing and talk
    I can see and laugh and wink and blink
    I can read and write and count and think
    I can jump and play and climb a tree
    I can twist and stretch and bend my knee.

    Answer: **I'm all of you!**

3. ***Identify the Skill Components:*** (List on board before class)

    1. Think of what you like about yourself (refer to the poem in #2).
    2. Think of what to say.
    3. How will you say it?
    4. Wait your turn.
    5. Say what you like about yourself. (Use complete sentences.)

4. ***Model the Skill:*** Teacher models the skill steps by saying something good about himself or herself, such as: **"I like to read a good book,"** or **"I like to play fair."**

5. ***Behavioral Rehearsal:***

    A. *Selection:* Teacher selects children to role play.

    B. *Role Play:* Give children the name of a famous person and/or profession. What might that person say about himself/herself. (What he/she likes about himself/herself) e.g., firefighter: "I work hard". . ."I help put out fires for people." Have children role play themselves doing a good deed.

    C. *Completion:* After each role play, reinforce correct behavior, identify inappropriate behaviors, and reenact role play with corrections. If there are no corrections, role play is complete.

    D. *Reinforcers:* Use material rewards, verbal praise, non-verbal expressions of approval (i.e., smile, pat, hug), and group reinforcement.

    E. *Discussion:* How does it make you feel when you say something nice about yourself?

6. ***Practice:*** Give children copies of the accompanying activity sheet, "Get in Shape—Feel Good," to complete in class. Check their drawings and discuss.

7. ***Independent Use:***

    A. Children tell classmates something they like about themselves.

    B. As homework, children tell an adult something they like about themselves. This can be the basis of a follow-up discussion another day.

8. ***Continuation:*** Teachers tell students to use healthy self-talk, such as, "I can do it," "I'm a good helper," "I can keep trying," etc.

CHILDREN'S LITERATURE
(Self-Image)

Hoffman, Mary. *Amazing Grace.* New York: Dial Books for Young Readers, 1991.

Kraus, Robert. *Leo the Late Bloomer.* New York: Harper Collins Children's Books, 1994.

Name _____   Date _____

GET IN SHAPE -- FEEL GOOD

Draw a picture of something that makes you feel good at home, school and play.

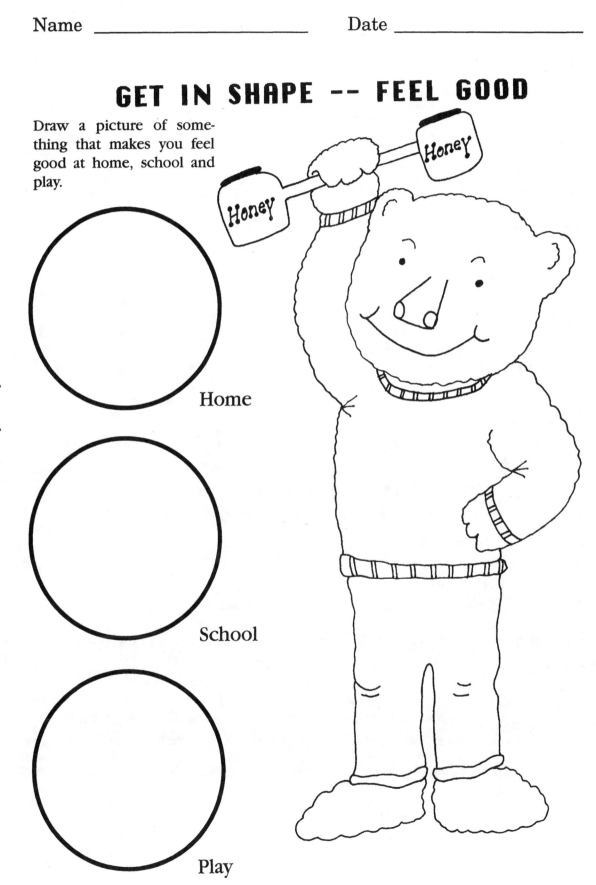

Home

School

Play

SOCIAL SKILL
Expressing Good Things About Oneself

Behavioral Objective: The children will state something they like about themselves when asked.

Directed Lesson:

1. *Establish the Need:* Review the idea that building a positive self-concept will build success academically and socially.

2. *Introduction:* Teacher reads story to class:

    "Once upon a time in the land of _____ school, there lived a tiny, brown dog. He had only one problem. He didn't know how very special he was. He knew how wise the owl was; how quickly ran the deer. The eagle flying high could see both far and near. The huge strong elephant never forgot a thing. The robin had a special song to sing. Would you help our special animal friend find something nice to say about himself/herself?"

    Have class give positive statements about dog. (Eg: He can bark, run, jump, fetch, wag his tail, etc.).

3. *Identify the Skill Components:* (List on board before class)

    1. Think of what you can do and what you like about yourself.
    2. Think of what to say.
    3. How will you say it?
    4. Wait your turn.
    5. Say what you like about yourself. (Use complete sentences.)

4. *Model the Skill:* The teacher says, **"I like myself because I teach children to read."**

5. *Behavioral Rehearsal:*

    A. *Selection:* Each child will pair off with the child they are sitting next to.

    B. *Role Play:* One child will ask the other, "What do you like about yourself?"

    C. *Completion:* After each role play, reinforce correct behavior, identify inappropriate behaviors, and reenact role play with corrections. If there are no corrections, role play is complete.

    D. *Reinforcers:* Ask the children to compliment each other on the positive things they said about themselves.

E. *Discussion:* Have children discuss how it feels to say positive things about themselves. Ask them if it was difficult to think of things to say. What advantages do they see in using this skill?

6. **Practice:** Have children complete one or more of the following four activity sheets.

   A. "Self-Praise Maze"—Do this activity together in class.

   B. "I Like Myself"—This individual activity can be done in class or at home.

   C. "Who Am I?"—The positive statements on the worksheet identify what a person with a certain occupation might say about himself. Have children write in their answers and check them in class.

   D. "The Good News Wishing Well"—Each child is to complete the activity individually in class or at home.

7. **Independent Use:**

   A. Have a home or school family member ask children to say something good about themselves every day for a week.

   B. The teacher will ask daily for volunteers to raise their hand and say something they like about themselves.

8. **Continuation:** Teacher tells children to say each day:

   > **"I like myself.**
   > **I like myself.**
   > **I *really* like myself."**

They can clap their hands together as they chant the words.

CHILDREN'S LITERATURE

Flournoy, Valerie. *The Patchwork Quilt.* New York: Dial Books for Young Readers, 1985.

Rylant, Cynthia. *Mr. Griggs' Work.*

Name _____   Date _____

SELF-PRAISE MAZE

Ken is sad because he cannot do his homework.
YOU can help.
Trace the path that Ken should take.
Then go back and read the words.

I need help!

Start here

Ask for help

Dead end

Give up!

Keep working

Feel sad

Do a good job

Thank you!

Name _____   Date _____

" I LIKE MYSELF . . . . I'M A VERY SPECIAL PERSON YOU SEE. I CAN SHOW YOU, 1, 2, 3."

Directions: Think of three things you can do that make YOU special. Use your crayons to show us in the three boxes below. Then, write a word in each box that tells HOW you feel.

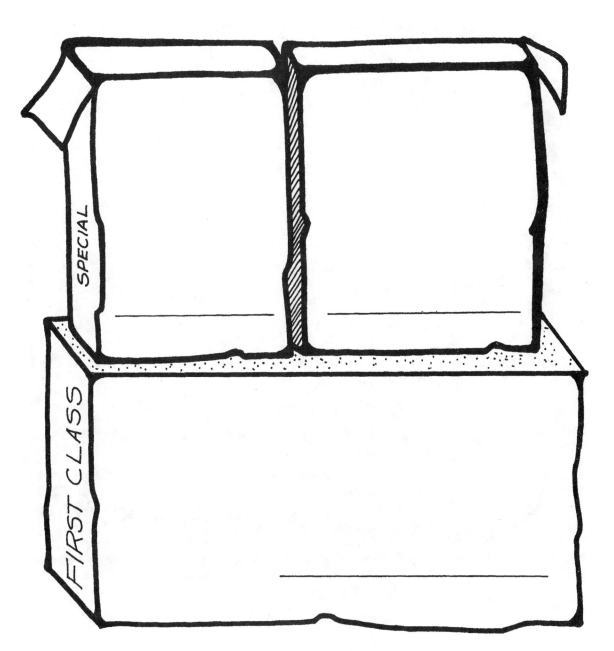

Name _____ Date _____

WHOOOOO AM I?

Ollie Owl wants to know the occupation of each person.
Can you help? Write the answer on the line.

1._____ I like myself because I heal sick people.

2._____ I like myself because I rescue people from fires.

3._____ I like myself because I help run our country.

4._____ I like myself because I help children learn.

5._____ I like myself because I create beautiful pictures.

6._____ I like myself because I make beautiful sounds come from an instrument.

7._____ I like myself because I can hit a ball and make a homerun.

8._____ I like myself because I can fix a broken tooth.

9._____ I like myself because I help keep a house or building clean.

10._____ I like myself because I let people know what is going on in the news every day.

Name _____ Date _____

Directions: This well is full of good news. Find three good things from the words in the well that tell something about YOU. Write them on the lines below the well. Oh, and don't forget to make a wish!

GOOD NEWS WISHING WELL

Helpful   Clean

Happy   Quiet

Singer   Neat

Like Animals

Respectful

Follow Directions

Hard Worker

Good Listener

Good Helper

_____

_____

_____

_____

_____

IMPROVING SELF-IMAGE

SOCIAL SKILL

Feeling Positive About Oneself

Behavioral Objective: The children will draw a picture showing themselves doing something that makes them feel proud.

Directed Lesson:

1. **Establish the Need:** Teacher initiates a discussion about the relevance and benefits of a positive attitude. Children need to learn that building a positive self-image will help build success in school and help them when dealing with people.

2. **Introduction:** Famous people were once young, just like them. They became successful because they thought they could accomplish great things. They liked many things about themselves. Use the following examples (place on board or signs):

   A. *Sally Ride:* "I was the first woman to go into space because I am a very good astronaut."

   B. *Bill Cosby:* "I created excellent T.V. programs because I have talent and knew I could do it."

   C. *Bruce Lee:* "I practiced many hours to become a great Karate expert. I liked the way it felt when I became a success."

3. **Identify the Skill Components:** (List on board before class)

   1. Think of things you can do that you like about yourself.
   2. Select one to express.
   3. Plan what you want to say.
   4. Raise your hand.
   5. Wait your turn.
   6. Make your positive statement.

4. **Model the Skill:** Teacher models the skill steps using examples of things she can do that she likes about herself.

5. **Behavioral Rehearsal:**

   A. *Selection:* Teacher selects children to role play. Try to have a least five children role play.

B. Role Play: Have children imagine they are other people and find something positive to say about themselves. *Examples:* Hulk Hogan, Martin Luther King. . . someone the class knows. Have children then role play themselves in pairs. One child asks the other, "What do you like about yourself?" His partner replies. They reverse roles.

C. Completion: After each role play, reinforce correct behavior, identify inappropriate behaviors, and reenact role play with corrections. If there are no corrections, role play is complete.

D. Reinforcers: Use verbal praise, tangible rewards, and physical displays of approval (i.e., hug, pat, smile, being selected as line leader, being chosen to select the book to be read aloud that day).

E. Discussion: Have children discuss the role plays and the corrections that were made. Ask the class what advantages they see in liking themselves. Discuss what problems the children have with the skill.

6. Practice:

1. Give children copies of the following activity sheet, "It's Me!" Each child writes something that he likes about himself and then illustrates it in the picture frame.

2. Next, distribute copies of the activity sheet entitled "The Daily Good News." Have each child complete the worksheet, then fasten it to the back of the first activity sheet with the child's self-portrait.

7. Independent Use:

A. Student tells classmate one thing he/she likes about her/himself during the week.

B. Student tells family member something he/she likes about her/himself. The child then writes it, has it signed by the family member, and returns it to school. During the next lesson the class will discuss what the advantages are of saying nice things about yourself.

8. Continuation: Teachers tell students to say each day:

"I like myself.

I like myself.

I *really* like myself."

They can clap their hands together as they chant the words. Teachers should continue pointing out the need for this skill as related situations arise.

CHILDREN'S LITERATURE

Carle, Eric. *The Mixed-up Chameleon.* New York: Harper Collins Children's Books, 1984.

Henkes, Kevin. *Crysanthemum.* New York: Wm. Morrow (Greenwillow), 1991.

Name _____ Date _____

IT'S ME!

On the following lines, write a sentence that tells something nice about yourself. Then, draw your picture inside the fancy frame.

_____

_____

_____

Name_____   Date _____

THE DAILY GOOD NEWS

EXTRA! EXTRA!

" I like myself," said

_____
(your name).

And, I will tell you why. It's because _____

_____

_____

_____

_____

I Can draw a circle around the words that describe me:

POLITE
NEAT
BIG
SMALL
KIND
FRIENDLY
HELPFUL

I AM MANY COLORS TODAY!

This is the color of my:

eyes _____

hair_____

shoes_____

hat_____

backpack_____

My favorite color is _____!

HERE I AM!

Draw your picture.

Editor's Name_____ Date_____

SOCIAL SKILL
Being Positive About Oneself

Behavioral Objective: The children will draw a self-portrait and write two positive statements about themselves on sentence strips to attach to the drawing.

Directed Lesson:

1. **Establish the Need:** Discuss with the students that everyone has good qualities and does something well. Even though it may not be done perfectly, it can still be done well.

2. **Introduction:** Ask students what one thing they enjoy and do well. Make a list on the chalkboard.

3. **Identify the Skill Components:** (List on board before class)

    1. Think about what you want to say.
    2. Raise your hand.
    3. Wait to be called on.
    4. Express your positive statement.

4. **Model the Skill:** Teacher will verbally make three different positive statements about self. "**I like the way I _____.**" "**I feel smart when _____.**" "**My favorite sport is _____.**"

5. **Behavioral Rehearsal:**

    A. *Selection:* Teacher will call on seven students to complete sentences written on the board. Then teacher will call on five more to start and complete their own positive statements.

    B. *Role Play:* Students will make positive statements about themselves.

    1. I'm terrific at _____.
    2. I like the way I _____.
    3. I am very good at _____.
    4. I like myself when I _____.
    5. My best subjects in school are _____.
    6. The sport that I'm best at is _____.
    7. I did a very nice thing for my mother. I _____.

    C. *Completion:* After each role play, reinforce correct behavior, identify inappropriate behaviors, and reenact role play with corrections. If there are no corrections, role play is complete.

    D. *Reinforcers:* verbal encouragement, tangible rewards, smile, giving class five extra minutes for silent reading, or for a game.

    E. *Discussion:* Have the children discuss the role plays and the corrections that were made. Ask the class the advantages of improving self-image.

6. **Practice:** Distribute copies of the following activity sheet, "My Sunny Day Favorites," for each child to complete in class.

7. **Independent Use:**

    A. Students are to write and draw pictures that reflect positive characteristics about themselves. Daily, teacher will ask them to share their favorite sentence or picture with the class.

    B. Teacher will praise students' efforts by verbally making positive statements about them during the day. Display in room (the statements and pictures by students).

8. **Continuation:** Teachers should continue pointing out the need for developing a positive attitude toward self as related situations arise.

CHILDREN'S LITERATURE

DeRegniers, Beatrice Schenk. *Sing a Song of Popcorn: Every Child's Book of Poems.* New York: Scholastic, 1988.

Ringgold, Faith. *Tar Beach.* New York: Crown Books for Young Readers, 1991.

Name_____   Date _____

MY SUNNY DAY FAVORITES

Write down your favorite activity or thing on each sun ray from #1 - #7.

1. Sport
2. Subject
3. Bird
4. T.V. Program
5. Game
6. Book
7. Flower

SOCIAL SKILL
Rewarding Oneself

Behavioral Objective: Children will identify three ways to reward themselves.

Directed Lesson:

1. ***Establish the Need:*** Teacher initiates a discussion about how building a positive self-image will help develop success in school.

2. ***Introduction:*** Ask the class the following questions:

   "How do you feel when someone rewards you?"

   "How do you feel when you did something good but nobody noticed?"

   "When your good behavior goes unnoticed, you can reward yourself. Tell yourself 'I did a great job' or 'I'm proud I _____.' Pat yourself on the back. Draw yourself an award and write a comment on it. Hang it on your desk.

3. ***Identify the Skill Components:*** (List on board before class)

   1. Identify what you think you did well.

   2. Reward yourself.

   3. Ask for confirmation from your friends and family.

4. ***Model the Skill:*** Teacher will model the skill by giving herself a pat on the back. She/he will say "I did a fine job of writing today." Teacher will demonstrate drawing an award for perfect attendance for the week and tape it on her desk.

5. ***Behavioral Rehearsal:***

   A. *Selection:* Teacher will select six students to role play each of the three rewards twice.

   B. *Role Play:* The teacher will direct two students to make awards to themselves showing good behavior in the library. Two students will make positive verbal comments about their own good behavior. All students will pat themselves on the back.

   C. *Completion:* After each role play, reinforce correct behavior, identify inappropriate behaviors, and reenact role play with corrections. If there are no corrections, role play is complete.

   D. *Reinforcers:* verbal encouragement, tangible rewards, nod approval and smile.

   E. *Discussion:* Have children discuss the role plays and the corrections that were made. Ask class to name the advantages of improving self-image.

6. ***Practice:*** Have each child draw a poster of him/herself showing his/her favorite activity.

7. ***Independent Use:*** Teacher will encourage students to make awards weekly and take them home to share with parents.

8. ***Continuation:*** To the tune of Mary Had a Little Lamb, end the day with a song:

> **"Today I did my very best**
> **Very best, very best**
> **Today I did my very best**
> **You did your best, too!"**

CHILDREN'S LITERATURE

Jonas, Ann. *Color Dance.* New York: Wm. Morrow (Greenwillow), 1989.

Pomerantz, Charlotte. *Flap Your Wings and Try.* New York: Wm. Morrow (Greenwillow), 1989.

SOCIAL SKILL

Accepting the Consequences of Our Actions

Behavioral Objective: The learner will admit wrongdoing and accept the consequences without complaining.

Directed Lesson:

1. ***Establish the Need:*** Teacher initiates a discussion about the relevance and benefits of the skill. Accepting consequences and fulfilling them without complaining will help to resolve the situation or conflict quickly.

2. ***Introduction:*** Teacher will read the following poem to the class.

    > **We had a problem**
    > **My friend and I**
    > **The teacher asked what happened**
    > **We told her truthfully and did not lie.**
    >
    > **We had broken a rule**
    > **We had run in the hall—**
    > **and since it was our third offense**
    > **We had to take the consequence.**

    Teacher will ask the following questions:

    ▶ **Were the students truthful about what they did?**

    ▶ **Should they have lied so they might not get in trouble?**

    ▶ **Should a person take the consequence for breaking a rule?**

    ▶ **Did the students complain about the consequence?**

    (Class rules should already be established—see Lessons 1 and 2.)

3. ***Identify the Skill Components:*** (List on board before class)

    1. Listen to what happened.
    2. Think about what you did.
    3. Admit it if you were wrong.
    4. Accept the consequences and don't complain.

4. ***Model the Skill:*** The teacher will model the skill by showing the class a sample of unacceptable papers turned in and an appropriate consequence for each student (e.g., for an unfinished paper, a paper with no name, a messy paper, etc.). **The teacher will use consequences established for the classroom prior to the lesson.**

5. ***Behavioral Rehearsal:***

    A. *Selection:* Teacher will select five students to role play the following skill steps for accepting consequences without complaining.

    B. *Role Play:*

        1. Not returning your homework.

        2. Leaving the room without permission.

        3. Eating candy in the classroom.

        4. Copying answers from another person's paper.

        5. Taking someone's property without permission.

    C. *Completion:* After each role play, reinforce correct behavior, identify inappropriate behaviors, and reenact role play with corrections. If there are no corrections, role play is complete.

    D. *Reinforcers:* Praise correct behavior verbally, for example:

        "I like the way _____ listened to what happened without interrupting."

        "I could tell that _____ was thinking about the rule she/he broke."

        "_____, you were right for admitting that you did break a classroom rule."

        "I noticed that _____ didn't complain when she/he heard the consequences of _____."

        "I thought the role play that _____ did was really good because they talked out their problem."

    E. *Discussion:* A discussion as to the correctness of the role play will follow after each role play situation.

6. ***Practice:*** Teacher will distribute the following activity sheet, "Don't Be Puzzled!!!," and read the directions. Tell the students to look at the key if they are having trouble putting together the puzzle. After completing the puzzle, read over the steps in accepting consequences.

7. ***Independent Use:***

    A. I would ask that each of you accept the consequences when you do not follow directions in the lunchroom. If one of the lunchroom aides tells you to do something because you broke a rule, are you going to cry, complain, or talk back? What will you do?

    B. Children will report on rules they have broken outside the classroom and the consequence they were given.

8. ***Continuation:*** Teachers will remind children that accepting the consequences of their wrongdoing usually resolves a problem quickly, as related situations arise.

Name _____   Date _____

DON'T BE PUZZLED!!!

Directions: Cut out the puzzle pieces and put them together. Add a tail and soon you will be flying high!

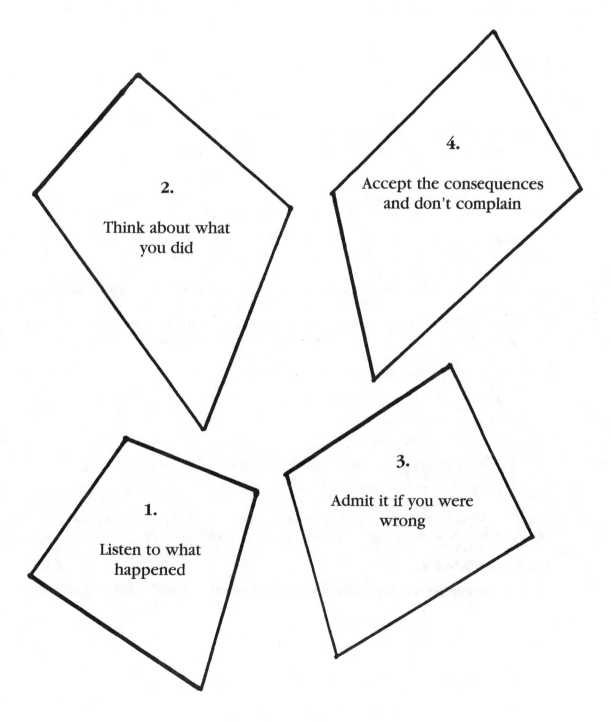

SOCIAL SKILL

Accepting Consequences for Breaking Rules

Behavioral Objective: The children will accept warranted consequences after doing something wrong.

Directed Lesson:

1. ***Establish the Need:*** Teacher initiates a discussion about the relevance and benefits of the skill. Social groups have rules for the benefit of the whole group. As a result, each individual benefits. To encourage compliance with the rules of the group, consequences have been devised for individuals who do not choose to comply.

2. ***Introduction:*** Teacher will say, **"Suppose you break the law and are caught by the police. When you go to court you are found guilty. You must then accept the consequences of your actions. What do you think some of the consequences might be?"**

   "Now suppose you are in your room at school and your teacher gives you a paper to color. You have lost your crayons, but you want to color the picture. You notice that your neighbor has a nice box of crayons, and while he is not looking, you take them and put them in your desk. Your teacher saw you take them and put them in your desk. She asks you about the crayons. What should you do? How do you think the teacher will feel about what you did? How do you think your neighbor, whose crayons you took, would feel? How would you feel if they were your crayons?"

3. ***Identify the Skill Components:*** (List on board before class)

   1. Listen to what you are accused of doing or saying.
   2. Think about what you did.
   3. Decide if it was wrong or right.
   4. If wrong, admit it.
   5. Accept the consequence.

4. ***Model the Skill:*** Teacher will model the skill by "breaking" one of the class rules; admitting the wrongdoing; and accepting the consequence posted for breaking that rule.

5. ***Behavioral Rehearsal:***

   A. *Selection:* Teacher selects four pairs of children to role play various situations.

B. *Role Play:* Have children role play situations in which they have done something wrong; have admitted it; and have decided they must accept the consequences of their actions. You can use classroom rules; examples of stealing or breaking property; talking back to adults in authority; running in the classroom, or whatever else is appropriate in your classroom.

C. *Completion:* After each role play, reinforce correct behavior, identify inappropriate behaviors, and reenact role play with corrections. If there are no corrections, role play is complete.

D. *Reinforcers:* verbal encouragement, tangible rewards, group reinforcement, and non-verbal expressions (i.e., hug, smile, pat).

E. *Discussion:* Have children discuss the role plays and the corrections that were made in each situation. Ask the class why it is necessary to have consequences for inappropriate actions. What would happen if people were allowed to do anything they wanted to?

6. *Practice:* Have students complete the activity sheet, "Rules & Consequences." Each rule that is listed must have a consequence that you think will stop children from breaking the rule. See "Suggestions to Teachers for Corrective Actions," on the next page, before applying consequences.

7. *Independent Use:*

A. Students must go to the end of the line for line-cutting.

B. Students will not be allowed to participate in group games if they exhibit inappropriate attitudes and actions.

C. Students must accept consequences of rule infractions and complete consequences without excessive complaining.

D. Students will do related incidents at home that relate to this skill.

8. *Continuation:* Teachers should continue pointing out the need for this skill as related situations arise. Stress the importance of good sportsmanship.

CHILDREN'S LITERATURE

Brown, Marcia. *Once a Mouse.* New York: Macmillan Children's Group, 1989.

Potter, Beatrix. *The Tale of Peter Rabbit.* New York: Bantam, 1984.

CHECK YOURSELF . . . HAVE YOU USED THESE?

Suggestions to Teachers for Corrective Actions

Things to do with individual students:

▶ Give children a writing assignment as a consequence for misbehavior.

▶ Hold a private conference with the student—away from his/her peers.

▶ In selected cases, hold a conference with the student in the presence of a peer who is respected by the class.

▶ Solicit the help of a parent.

Things to do for the entire class:

▶ Expose students to role models, prominent and contemporary speakers.

▶ Assign group responsibilities.

▶ Be aware of the importance of class structure, student groupings, and student seating.

▶ Post expectations/rules/consequences in the classroom.

▶ Develop and use a "good behavior" chart.

Help yourself to improve classroom discipline.

Name _____ Date _____

RULES AND CONSEQUENCES

Directions: Each rule listed below must have a consequence. Read the rule and write a consequence that you think would be helpful in keeping someone from breaking the rule.

_____

CONSEQUENCES are what you have to accept as a result of breaking a rule. For example: if you break a classroom rule three times, the consequence will be a note sent home and a phone call to your parents to discuss your behavior.

_____

RULE #1:   Do not run in the room or in the hall.

Consequence: _____

_____

RULE #2:   Do not throw food in the lunchroom.

Consequence:

_____

_____

RULE #3:   Do not take another person's property without permission.

Consequence: _____

_____

RULE #4:   Do not stand up or get out of your seat if the bus is moving.

Consequence: _____

_____

RULE #5:   Keep your hands, feet, and objects to yourself.

Consequence: _____

_____

ACCEPTING CONSEQUENCES

SOCIAL SKILL

Accepting Consequences Without Complaining

Behavioral Objective: The children will admit wrongdoing and accept the consequences with good sportsmanship.

Directed Lesson:

1. **Establish the Need:** Teacher reviews the importance of everyone accepting the consequences of his/her own actions. The advantage is that the problem is resolved quickly. By accepting consequences, we can move on to something different.

2. **Introduction:** Teacher will read the following story:

   "Once there was a student named Joe who went to (_____) school. Joe liked to play games, but he could not stand to lose. If he lost, he would become very angry and accuse the other players of cheating. He would try to keep the other players from enjoying the game. When Joe acted this way, his teacher would send him to the 'time out' area. If Joe accepted these consequences without complaining, he would spend a short time isolated. However, if he complained, he would have to spend a longer time by himself.

   "How do you think Joe felt when he was in the 'time out' area and could see the other children enjoying the game? What do you think happened if Joe complained about his consequences? How do you think the teacher felt?"

3. **Identify the Skill Components:** (List on board before class)

   1. Listen to what you are accused of.
   2. Think about what you did.
   3. Decide that it was wrong.
   4. Admit that it was wrong.
   5. Accept the consequence.

4. **Model the Skill:** Teacher will model the behavior by "breaking" one of the class rules; admit he/she was wrong; and accept the consequence without complaining.

5. **Behavioral Rehearsal:**

   A. *Selection:* Teacher selects five pairs of children to role play.

   B. *Role Play:* The children will role play situations in which they admit doing something wrong, accept the consequences without complaining, and fulfill the consequence. Use situations that are appropriate to your classroom rules and expectations.

C. *Completion:* After each role play, reinforce correct behavior, identify inappropriate behaviors, and reenact role play with corrections. If there are no corrections, role play is complete.

D. *Reinforcers:* verbal encouragement, tangible rewards, group reinforcement.

E. *Discussion:* Have children discuss the role plays and the corrections that were made. Ask the class why it is better to admit your wrongdoing and accept the consequences quietly than to complain about them.

6. **Practice:** Have the children complete and discuss the following activity sheet, "Accepting Consequences." The students will answer how they feel about the various consequences listed and what they think would be the appropriate one.

7. **Independent Use:**

A. Children will use the skill during all classroom and school activities.

B. Children will discuss incidents that have occurred at home or in other areas of the school.

8. **Continuation:** Teachers should continue to point out the importance of accepting the consequences of our own actions as related situations occur.

CHILDREN'S LITERATURE

Frog Princess: A Russian Folktale. Retold by Patrick Lewis. New York: Dial Books for Young Readers, 1994.

Yorinks, Arthur. *Hey, Al!* New York: Farrar, Straus & Giroux, 1989.

Name _____   Date _____

ACCEPTING CONSEQUENCES

Directions: Answer each question in the space provided. Then discuss your answers with classmates.

1. YOU did not bring your homework to school, so during recess you will be asked to do it **again**. How do you **feel** about this consequence? _____

    _____

    _____

2. YOU borrowed your best friend's radio and dropped it. Now it is broken! What consequence do you think would be fair? _____

    _____

    _____

3. YOU are playing a game and are losing. Next, you throw the game pieces on the floor. You are sent to the "time out" area for five minutes to think about the situation. When you return, what words will you use to apologize for your action? _____

    _____

    _____

4. YOU were throwing rocks and hit your father's car. What should the consequence be?

    _____

    _____

5. YOU got angry with your friend, lost your self-control, and tore up her/his homework. The teacher had you re-copy the homework. What will you say to yourself **IF** you are tempted to do this again? _____

    _____

IF YOU ACT FIRST AND THINK LATER, YOU MAY GET INTO TROUBLE AND HAVE TO TAKE THE CONSEQUENCES. WHAT ADVICE WILL YOU GIVE TO THE BIRD IN THE SPACE BELOW?

© 1995 by Society for Prevention of Violence

SOCIAL SKILL
Formulating Verbal Apologies

Behavioral Objective: When a child has misbehaved, he/she will accept the consequences without complaining and give apology.

Directed Lesson:

1. **Establish the Need:** Teacher initiates a discussion about how accepting consequences shows others that you are responsible for your actions.

2. **Introduction:** Ask the following questions and list answers on the board. **"What types of consequences do you think are fair for improper behavior?" "How should a student behave when consequences of actions are called for?"**

3. **Identify the Skill Components:** (List on board before class)

    1. Accept the consequence for inappropriate behavior without complaining.
    2. Determine what to say.
    3. Give an apology.

4. **Model the Skill:** Teacher will select a student to role play a teacher and to read a sample consequence to him/her concerning a rule he/she broke. Teacher will role play acceptance of the consequence without complaining, and give a verbal apology.

5. **Behavioral Rehearsal:**

    A. *Selection:* Teacher will select six students to read consequences and six students who will accept them.

    B. *Role Play:* One student will read the rule that was broken and another student will state the consequence. The student will then accept the consequence and give verbal apology.

    The following situations will be written on cards by teacher:

    1. Students will have to stay in for recess if they fight in the lunchroom.
    2. Students who push ahead in a line have to go to the end of the line.
    3. Students will have to wash all desk tops after school if they have scribbled on their desks.
    4. Students will have to go to another class for two periods if they have been disrespectful to an adult.

85

    C. *Completion:* After each role play, reinforce correct behavior, identify inappropriate behaviors, and reenact role play with corrections. If there are no corrections, role play is complete.

    D. *Reinforcers:* Provide verbal encouragement, tangible rewards, or a smile to show approval.

    E. *Discussion:* Have students discuss the role plays and corrections that were made. Ask class what the advantages are of accepting consequences.

6.   *Practice:* Hand out copies of the following "Word Match" activity sheet for children to complete in class. Check their work and review the words.

7.   *Independent Use:* Students relate what consequences they had on actions they took outside of the school setting.

8.   *Continuation:* As situations arise, teachers should remind children that giving a verbal apology shows that we accept responsibility for our own actions.

CHILDREN'S LITERATURE

Estes, Eleanor. *The Hundred Dresses.* New York: Harcourt Brace, 1974.

Name _____   Date _____

WORD MATCH

Directions: *Read the words in the Word Bank. Then, on the line next to the word list, write the word that means the same.*

1. consequence   _____

2. accept   _____

3. behavior   _____

4. punishment   _____

5. improper   _____

6. fair   _____

7. complaint   _____

8. explanation   _____

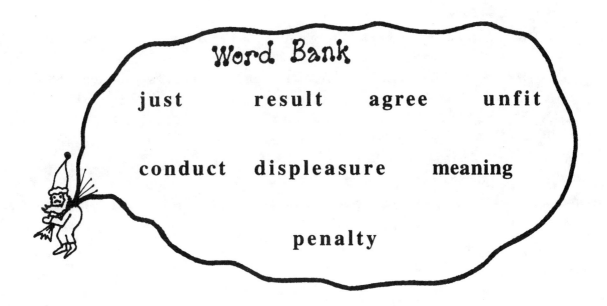

Word Bank

just   result   agree   unfit

conduct   displeasure   meaning

penalty

SOCIAL SKILL

Accepting Consequences for Accidents

Behavioral Objective: Children will report to teacher when an item is damaged, and explain how the damage occurred. Emphasize safety in the classroom.

Directed Lesson:

1. **Establish the Need:** Discuss the importance of accepting that sometimes accidents happen that damage another's property. Even though admitting you caused the accident doesn't correct the damage, further false accusations towards you could make the situation worse.

2. **Introduction:** Ask the students the following questions and list the responses on the board. **"What happens if you don't tell the teacher?" What happens if you tell the teacher?"**

3. **Identify the Skill Components:** (List on board before class)

    1. Think about how the accident occurred.
    2. Tell the teacher.
    3. Apologize.
    4. Ask permission to clean up.

4. **Model the Skill:** Teacher will model a student's explanation for knocking down a plant, such as: "Mrs. Smith when I walked by the plant, my hand swung and knocked it down. I'm sorry. I'll be careful next time. May I clean the floor?"

5. **Behavioral Rehearsal:**

    A. *Selection:* Teacher will select eight students to read examples describing accidents, then give explanations.

    B. *Role Play:* Each student will read an example aloud to class and compose a verbal explanation and an apology. The following examples may be written on cards or on the board:

       1. Knocking books off the shelf.
       2. Spilling water on the floor.
       3. Ripping a page in the text.
       4. Tearing a sheet off the bulletin board.
       5. Marking a wall with crayon.
       6. Spilling the pencil sharpener contents.

7. Kicking the person in front of you.

8. Stepping on someone's foot as you pass by.

C. *Completion:* After each role play, reinforce correct behavior, identify inappropriate behaviors, and reenact role play with corrections. If there are no corrections, role play is complete.

D. *Reinforcers:* verbal praise, smile and nod head to show approval. Keep a "Safe Classroom" chart, and give stickers after daily assessment with class.

E. *Discussion:* Have children discuss role plays and corrections made. Ask class why it is important to tell an adult if something has been damaged by him/her.

6. *Practice:* Distribute copies of the following "Three Cheers for Safety Cut-Out Badge" and have children fill in their names.

7. *Independent Use:* Teacher will ask students to share accidental occurrences that happened outside of class, and how the student followed up with an explanation and resolution.

8. *Continuation:* Teachers should remind children of the importance of reporting accidents to the teacher or other adult as related situations arise.

Name _____ Date _____

THREE CHEERS FOR SAFETY CUT-OUT BADGE

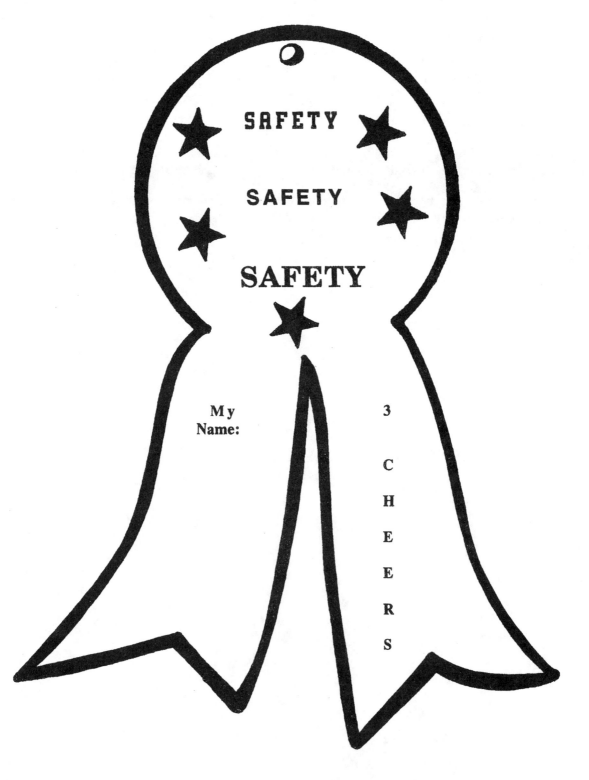

SOCIAL SKILL
Making Wise Choices

Behavioral Objective: The children will identify the consequences of behavior involving a wrongdoing.

Directed Lesson:

1. **Establish the Need:** It is important to know the consequences of misbehavior to help people decide if the action is worth taking.

2. **Introduction:** "Andy, do you remember what to do when encouraged by a friend to do something wrong? Yes! You think, say no, and walk away. What might happen if you decide to leave the classroom without permission?"

3. **Identify the Skill Components:** (Place on board before class)

   1. Learn the rules at home and at school.

   2. Learn what happens when you break these rules. (Consequences)

   3. Decide what you can do to avoid breaking rules? (Choose wisely)

4. **Model the Skill:** Teacher will model the skill by saying **"Jan, I'm glad you realize that when you put your feet out in the aisle you could cause someone to trip and fall. Try to remember that all the time. Sit straight with both feet in front of you."**

5. **Behavioral Rehearsal:**

   A. *Selection:* Teacher selects four pairs of children to role play.

   B. *Role Play:*

      1. Lisa and Vera will be made to stay after school for playing hooky.

      2. Tony gets a suspension from the teacher for breaking a classroom rule.

      3. Bob and Jim get into a fight on the playground and have to stay after school.

      4. Jack and Joe walk down the hall and decide to play in the restroom instead of returning to the room.

   C. *Completion:* After each role play, reinforce correct behavior, identify inappropriate behaviors, and reenact role play with corrections. If there are no corrections, role play is complete.

     D. *Reinforcers:*

        1. **"Good, I'm glad you understand that it's wrong."**

        2. **"You did the right thing."**

     E. *Discussion:* Have children discuss the role plays. Stress that before we do something wrong we need to consider the consequences of what we do. If we choose to do it anyway, we have to be prepared to accept the consequences of our choice.

6. ***Practice:*** Give children copies of the accompanying activity page, "Aim for the Sky." Have them write good school rules on the kites, and the possible consequences of not following the rules.

7. ***Independent Use:*** Have children discuss the role plays. Stress that before we do something wrong we need to consider the consequences of what we do. If we choose to do it anyway, we have to be prepared to accept the consequences of the choice.

8. ***Continuation:*** Teachers should continue to point out the importance of knowing the likely consequences of wrongdoing so that each of us can act wisely.

CHILDREN'S LITERATURE

Barrett, Judi. *Animals Should Definitely Not Wear Clothing.* New York: Macmillan Children's Group, 1988.

Brett, Jan. *Berlioz the Bear.* New York: Putnam Publishing Group, 1991.

Name _____ Date _____

AIM FOR THE SKY

Directions: Write a good school rule on each kite. IF THE RULES ARE NOT FOLLOWED, write the consequences on the three lines below the kites.

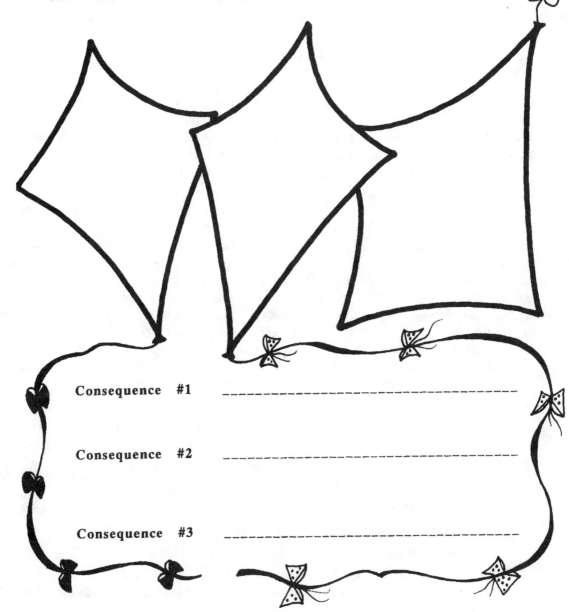

Consequence #1 _____

Consequence #2 _____

Consequence #3 _____

SOCIAL SKILL
Solving a Problem by Sharing

Behavioral Objective: The children will identify the problem and solve it, after considering a number of alternatives.

Directed Lesson:

1. **Establish the Need:** Teacher initiates a discussion about the relevance and benefits of the skill. Problem solving will build success academically and socially by restricting the number of conflicts, thereby increasing learning time. When children try to resolve their own conflicts, they become more self-sufficient and it provides increased time for learning.

2. **Introduction:** Read the following story aloud:

    "Two bunnies named Oscar and Curley were hopping to _____ school. As they passed Farmer Frank's farm they found three dollars. The farmer said that they could buy three jumbo carrots. Oscar and Curley were very excited and hopped as fast as they could to school. They sat through Mrs. Fone's health class and were finally ready for lunch. Both bunnies sat under a large tree and each ate a jumbo carrot. But they were still hungry and they only had one carrot left. They started arguing about who would eat it and made so much noise that Mrs. Fone came over to see what was wrong. The bunnies realized that it would be better to solve their own problem rather than have the teacher solve it. They quickly and quietly thought about different ways to settle the problem and decided on the best one . . . sharing the carrot. Mrs. Fone was proud of these two problem-solvers."

    Teacher asks class: **"Why were the bunnies arguing?"**

    "Why is it a good idea to settle your own problems?"

3. **Identify the Skill Components:** (List on board before class)

    1. Identify the problem. (Identification)
    2. Identify different ways to solve it. (Possible Solutions)
    3. Decide what can happen after trying each solution. (Possible Outcomes)
    4. Decide what is the best thing to do. (Decision Making)
    5. If it doesn't work, learn to try another solution. (Evaluation)

4. **Model the Skill:** Teacher models the skill steps by pretending to be a student who wants to use the yardstick at the same time another student wants to use it. Select a student to role play the other student, and work through the five skill steps listed above.

5. ***Behavioral Rehearsal:***

    A. *Selection:* Teacher will select three pairs of children to role play.

    B. *Role Play:* Children will role play the following situations of problem solving.

        1. One child broke another child's pencil.

        2. The teacher gave two children one box of crayons to use.

        3. One child bumps into another child.

    C. *Completion:* After each role play, reinforce correct behavior, identify inappropriate behaviors, and reenact role play with corrections. If there are no corrections, role play is complete.

    D. *Reinforcers:* Praise those students who are successful in their role plays. Encourage others to reenact correctly. Bring in puppets so that children can use them for role play.

    E. *Discussion:* Have children discuss the role plays and the difficulties encountered when using problem-solving skills.

6. ***Practice:*** Give children copies of the following activity sheet, "The Umbrella Problem Solvers," to complete. After checking children's work, have them color the umbrella.

7. ***Independent Use:*** Children will think of alternatives for a solution to a problem at home, decide on the best one, and report to class.

8. ***Continuation:*** Teacher tells children to think of different ways to solve a problem peacefully, as related situations arise.

CHILDREN'S LITERATURE
(Folktales for Problem Solving)

Brett, Jan. *Beauty and the Beast.* Boston: Houghton Mifflin (Clarion), 1990.

McKissack, Patricia C. *Flossie and the Fox.* New York: Dial Books for Young Readers, 1986.

Name _____ Date _____

THE UMBRELLA PROBLEM SOLVERS

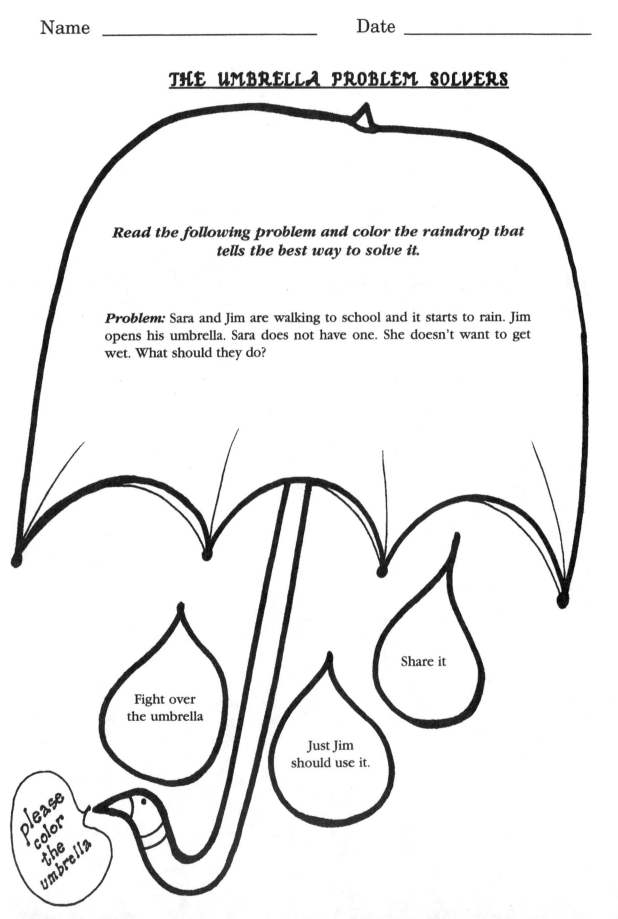

Read the following problem and color the raindrop that tells the best way to solve it.

Problem: Sara and Jim are walking to school and it starts to rain. Jim opens his umbrella. Sara does not have one. She doesn't want to get wet. What should they do?

Fight over the umbrella

Just Jim should use it.

Share it

please color the umbrella

SOCIAL SKILL
Using Problem-Solving Strategies

Behavioral Objective: The children will think of alternatives to a problem and decide on the best one.

Directed Lesson:

1. **Establish the Need:** Establish the fact that problem solving will build success academically and socially by restricting the number of conflicts, thereby increasing learning time. When children try to resolve their own conflicts, they become more self-sufficient and it frees the teacher to work with children in an atmosphere designed for learning.

2. **Introduction:** Read this poem to the class:

    > **Problems, problems every day.**
    > **Solve them in a friendly way.**
    > **Do we talk or do we fight?**
    > **Try to do whatever's right.**
    > **If we talk the problem out,**
    > **We won't have to yell and shout.**
    > **If we solve it on our own,**
    > **We will feel that we have grown.**

3. **Identify the Skill Components:** (List on board before class)

    1. Identify the problem.
    2. Identify different ways to solve it.
    3. Find out what can happen after trying each solution.
    4. Decide what is the best thing to do.
    5. If it doesn't work, learn to try another solution.

4. **Model the Skill:** Teacher models the five skill steps and decides what to try as a solution when the door to the room is stuck.

5. **Behavioral Rehearsal:**

    A. *Selection:* Teacher will select two *pairs* of children and two *individual* children to role play.

97

    B. *Role Play:* The two *pairs* of children will role play solving the following problems: (1.) having one ruler between them; (2.) wanting to take the same book from the library. The two *individual* children will role play: (1.) trying to find a quiet place to do homework; (2.) what to do if they accidentally tear their paper with hand-written notes.

    C. *Completion:* After each role play, reinforce correct behavior, identify inappropriate behaviors, and reenact role play with corrections. If there are no corrections, role play is complete.

    D. *Reinforcers:* Praise children who were able to think of positive solutions to the problems they were given. Make badges that say: "I'm a problem solver" and distribute them to the class.

    E. *Discussion:* Children should discuss what alternative solutions they can use to solve the problems from the role plays.

6. **Practice:** Give children copies of the following activity sheet, "Find the Best Solution," to complete in class.

7. **Independent Use:**

    A. Discuss the way that a T.V. character was able to solve a problem without fighting.

    B. Discuss what school problems the children were able to solve during the previous week.

8. **Continuation:** Teachers should encourage children to come up with their own creative solutions to conflicts as related situations arise.

CHILDREN'S LITERATURE

Brown, Marc, *Arthur's Teacher Trouble.* New York: Joy Street Books, 1989.

Name _____   Date _____

FIND THE BEST SOLUTION

Directions: **Draw a line to match each problem to the**
<u>best</u> solution.

PROBLEM	SOLUTION

1. **Two children have**
   one box of crayons.

    A.   **TAKE TURNS**

2. **A girl lost her math**
   worksheet.

    B.   **SHARE**

3. **A boy got mud**
   on his pants.

    C.   **ASK FOR A**
         NEW PAPER

4. **Two children want to use**
   the sink at the same time.

    D.   **WASH THEM**

SOCIAL SKILL
Thinking of Alternative Solutions

Behavioral Objective: The children will think of alternative solutions to a problem and decide on the best one.

Directed Lesson:

1. **Establish the Need:** Teacher initiates a discussion about the relevance and benefits of the skill. It is important for children to learn the skill of finding alternative methods of dealing with problems. It gives them practice in finding the best way to deal with specific situations. It helps them resolve conflicts more efficiently and calmly. When children learn that they have various ways to deal with a problem, they can pick and choose without feeling forced to accept one method. Often the most obvious solution is not the best one. Practicing problem-solving techniques promotes the children's ability to use the skill and helps them decide when to use it.

2. **Introduction:** "There are different kinds of problems that we must be able to solve. There are math problems, such as . . . What is five plus five? And spelling problems, such as . . . How do you spell mother? And nutrition problems, such as . . . What kind of healthy lunch should I eat today? There are also other problems that you might have in school, at home, and with other people. It is important to solve problems as peacefully as possible. Once you realize what the problem is, you must follow through with the problem-solving formula below (#3)."

3. **Identify the Skill Components:** (List on board before class)

    1. Identify the problem.
    2. Identify different ways to solve the problem.
    3. Learn what can happen after trying each one.
    4. Find out what is the best thing to do.
    5. If it doesn't work, learn to try some other solution.

4. **Model the Skill:** The teacher models the skill steps by showing the class how to work out the following problem . . . a homework assignment is due and the student has not finished the work.

5. **Behavioral Rehearsal:**

    A. *Selection:* Teacher selects six children to role play.

B. *Role Play:*

1. Two children role play wanting to sit in the same seat during lunch.
2. Two children role play wanting to take materials to the principal's office.
3. A child role plays spilling milk on the kitchen floor of his/her home.
4. A child role plays forgetting to bring in his/her homework, even though it was completed.

C. *Completion:* After each role play, reinforce correct behavior, identify inappropriate behaviors, and reenact role play with corrections. If there are no corrections, role play is complete.

D. *Reinforcers:* Verbal encouragement from teacher and rest of class; and a certificate that says that the holder is a good problem solver.

E. *Discussion:* Have children discuss the role plays and the corrections that were made. Ask them to describe the types of problems they have encountered when using the skill.

6. **Practice:** Give children copies of the following activity page, "What's the Best Solution?" Children will reach a decision about the best solution for each problem.

7. **Independent Use:**

A. Have students write down examples of how and when they used the problem solving techniques in their home. Ask a parent to read and sign.

B. Have children share examples of problems solved at home during daily sharing time.

8. **Continuation:** Encourage children to come up with several different ways to solve a problem as related situations arise.

CHILDREN'S LITERATURE

Blaine, Marge. *The Terrible Thing That Happened at Our House.* New York: Scholastic, 1991.

Milhous, Katherine and Alice Dalgiesh. *The Turnip; An Old Russian Folktale.* New York: Putnam Publishing Group, 1990.

Name _____   Date _____

WHAT'S THE BEST SOLUTION?

Directions: Write in what you think the best solution is to each problem.

PROBLEM #1   John forgot his lunch.

_____

_____

_____

PROBLEM #2   Jane broke her last pencil.

_____

_____

_____

PROBLEM #3   Pat and Mike found a quarter.

_____

_____

_____

PROBLEM #4   Ronnie and Nancy want to sit next to the teacher on the bus.

_____

_____

_____

SOCIAL SKILL
Applying Problem-Solving Techniques

Behavioral Objective: The children will think of problem solving alternatives and decide on the best course of action.

Directed Lesson:

1. **Establish the Need:** Review the concept that problem solving techniques are important to learn so that children have alternatives for dealing with various situations. They need to be able to solve some of their own problems and to be able to decide when to use these techniques. Children need practice in making choices and selecting the best possible solution. Learning to solve the problem more peacefully and fairly will help lessen the impact of the problem.

2. **Introduction:**   What's the problem, do you know?

    Solve it now or it will grow.

    Think of ways to end it fast.

    Pick the best so it will last.

    Have this poem written on the board and read by the class. Ask the class to give reasons why it is important to solve problems quickly and fairly. Lead them in a discussion of why it is helpful to be able to think of alternative behaviors to solve problems.

3. **Identify the Skill Components:** (List on board before class)

    1. Identify the problem.
    2. Identify different ways to solve the problem.
    3. Decide what can happen after trying each solution.
    4. Decide what is the best thing to do.
    5. If it doesn't work, try something else.

4. **Model the Skill:** Teacher models the skill steps by showing the class that there are different alternative solutions to the following problems, and selecting the best one . . .

    Problem: The teacher pretends to break the heel of one shoe. Teacher discusses possible solutions (i.e., paste heel, put on another pair and have heel repaired properly).

5. **Behavioral Rehearsal:**

    A. *Selection:* Teacher selects children as needed and as time allows.

103

B. *Role Play:* Children role play situations that were written for the previous lesson's role plays.

C. *Completion:* After each role play, reinforce correct behavior, identify inappropriate behaviors, and reenact role play with corrections. If there are no corrections, role play is complete.

D. *Reinforcers:* verbal praise by teacher and students alike. Class will listen to a fanciful folktale to determine how the character solved a problem.

E. *Discussion:* Have children discuss the types of problems that they are called on to solve in the home and school. Use the examples from the role playing to select the best solutions for these problems. Stress the importance of thinking about alternatives before making a decision.

6. *Practice:* Give students copies of the following activity sheet, "Problems & Solutions." Have each child list three alternatives for each problem, then write the solution he or she considers to be the best.

7. *Independent Use:* Have students write about one difficult problem that they had to solve at home. List the alternatives that they thought about, the consequences for each one, and how and why they decided to use one of the alternatives.

8. *Continuation:* Teachers should continue to encourage children to come up with problem-solving alternatives as related situations arise.

CHILDREN'S LITERATURE

Aardema, Verna. *Who's in Rabbit's House?* New York: Dial Books for Young Readers, 1977.

Uchida, Yoshiko. *The Dancing Kettle.* Berkeley, CA: Creative Arts Books, 1986.

Name _____   Date _____

PROBLEMS AND SOLUTIONS

Directions: List three alternative solutions for each problem. Write down which you consider to be the best solution to each problem and why you think so.

PROBLEM: Janet was running with her mother's vase and broke it.

Alternative Solutions:

1. _____

_____

2. _____

_____

3. _____

_____

Best Solution:

_____

_____

PROBLEM: Rhoda and Dorothy both wanted to eat the last cookie.

Alternative Solutions:

1. _____

_____

2. _____

_____

3. _____

_____

Best Solution:

_____

_____

SOCIAL SKILL
Avoiding Fights

Behavioral Objective: The children will respond to physical assault (hitting) by walking away, diverting attention or telling an adult.

Directed Lesson:

1. ***Establish the Need:*** Teacher reviews the importance of knowing what to do when someone teases or tries to start a fight. Discuss the consequences of hitting back and getting into fights. Fighting *does not* solve problems.

2. ***Introduction:*** Ask children, **"If someone wanted to start a fight with you in the lunchroom, what would you do?"** After getting several possible solutions, introduce the following steps for preventing physical assault.

3. ***Identify the Skill Components:*** (List on board before class)

    1. Do not fight.
    2. Discuss and walk away.
    3. Change subject or play elsewhere.
    4. Tell an adult.
    5. Shake hands.

4. ***Model the Skill:*** Teacher models the skill steps. Teacher demonstrates a technique for handling the situation in the lunchroom. Teacher informs children that fighting doesn't solve the problem.

5. ***Behavioral Rehearsal:***

    A. *Selection:* Select four pairs of children to role play the following situations:

    B. *Role Play:*

        1. David, when playing kickball with Joe, amiss to start a fight when called out at first base.
        2. Kim shoves Sarah and throws her papers on the floor.
        3. George tries to push Sam out of the line.
        4. Jane bumps Liz to get her out of the lunch line.

    C. *Completion:* After each role play, reinforce correct behavior, identify inappropriate behaviors, and reenact role play with corrections. If there are no corrections, role play is complete.

D. *Reinforcers:* Class receives a big award posted on the classroom door if they stay out of fights at school, on the bus and at the bus stop, etc., for a period of one week.

E. *Discussion:* Have the children discuss the steps for avoiding fights. Who can name the steps? Discuss any difficulties they have with developing and carrying out this skill.

6. ***Practice:*** Distribute copies of the following activity sheet, "The Pizza Problem-Solving Formula." Ask children to fill in the pizza slices with appropriate behaviors to avoid fighting.

7. ***Independent Use:*** Children write about situations where they did choose an alternative to fighting. Have them relate the situations to incidents outside the classroom.

8. ***Continuation:*** Teacher should remind children that fighting does not solve problems, and often makes them worse. They should think about this as related situations occur.

CHILDREN'S LITERATURE

Lester, Julius. *The Tales of Uncle Remus: The Adventures of Br'er Rabbit.* New York: Dial Books for Young Readers, 1987.

Name _____   Date _____

"THE PIZZA PROBLEM-SOLVING FORMULA"

Drake is looking for the perfect problem-solving pizza! On each pizza slice, write ONE WAY to avoid fights. Then decorate your delicious pizza.

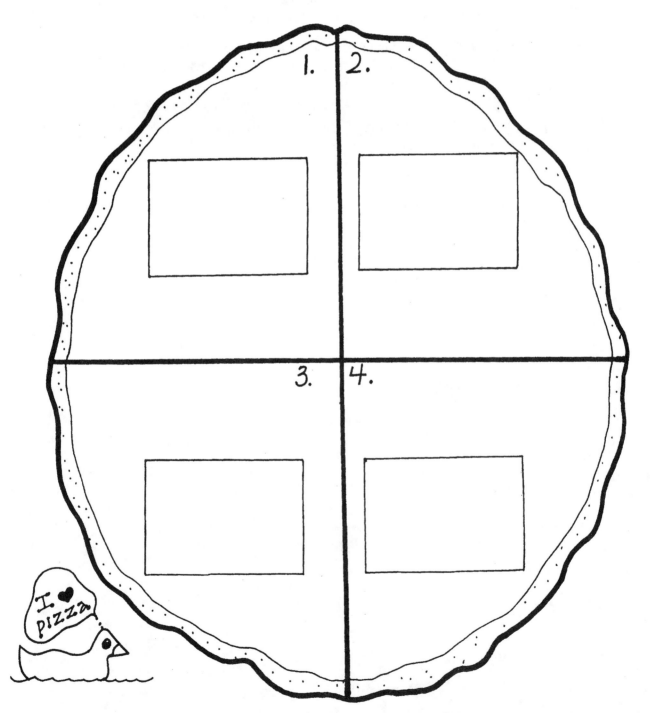

SOCIAL SKILL
Expressing Anger Verbally

Behavioral Objective: Student will express anger in a nonaggressive manner.

Directed Lesson:

1. **Establish the Need:** Teacher initiates a discussion with the following comment: **"If we want others to listen we need to express anger in a nonaggressive manner."**

2. **Introduction:** Ask student, **"If you accidentally spilled someone's juice at lunch, which of the following responses would you prefer and why? 'Hey you dummy, you spilled my juice,' or 'You have upset me because you spilled my juice.'"**

    Discuss reasons for preferred responses.

3. **Identify the Skill Components:** (List on board before class)

    1. Identify reason for anger.
    2. Think how to phrase anger nonaggressively.
    3. Express verbally.

4. **Model the Skill:** Teacher will model two nonaggressive comments. "I'm upset to hear that you were very noisy in the lunchroom," and "I find myself getting angry when I have to ask you to pay attention when I'm speaking."

5. **Behavioral Rehearsal:**

    A. *Selection:* Teacher will select ten students to role play.

    B. *Role Play:* Student will read one sentence off the board and pretend that that action happened to him/her and then give a nonaggressive comment.

    1. Someone stepped on your new shoes.
    2. You are interrupted when reading.
    3. Someone takes your pencil without asking.
    4. Your friend returns your new brush but it's dirty.
    5. A classmate has called you goofy.
    6. A classmate knocks over your books.
    7. The person behind you pushes you.
    8. The person next to you keeps talking while you're working.
    9. Someone slams the door.
    10. A friend forgets to keep a promise to call you.

    C. *Completion:* After each role play, reinforce correct behavior, identify inappropriate behaviors, and reenact role play with corrections. If there are no corrections, role play is complete.

    D. *Reinforcers:* Teacher will motivate students by rewarding them with a star on a "Social Skill Chart" and also with verbal praise.

    E. *Discussion:* Have children discuss the role plays and the corrections that were made. Encourage class to name the advantages of expressing anger in a nonaggressive manner.

6. ***Practice:*** Give students copies of the following activity sheet, "Feeling Happy/Feeling Angry: Storybook Characters," to complete in class. Children will identify five characters who were angry and explain why, then five characters who were happy and explain why.

7. ***Independent Use:***

    A. Students relate/write about incidents of self-control outside of the classroom.

    B. Teacher will ask students to share nonaggressive actions at the end of the day.

8. ***Continuation:*** As related situations arise, the teacher should stress the importance of expressing anger verbally, not physically.

CHILDREN'S LITERATURE

Prelutsky, Jack. *Tyrannosaurus Was a Beast: Dinosaur Poems.* New York: Morrow (Mulberry), 1992.

Wilhelm, Hans. *Tyrone the Horrible.* New York: Scholastic, 1992.

Name _____   Date _____

FEELING HAPPY/FEELING ANGRY   STORY BOOK CHARACTERS

List five storybook characters who were angry, and explain why.

Angry storybook characters: Why were they angry?

1. _____   _____

2. _____   _____

3. _____   _____

4. _____   _____

5. _____   _____

Now list five storybook characters who were happy, and why.

Happy storybook characters: Why were they happy?

1. _____   _____

2. _____   _____

3. _____   _____

4. _____   _____

5. _____   _____

SOCIAL SKILL

Completing an Assigned Job

Behavioral Objective: The children will be able to neatly complete an assignment given by the teacher or another adult.

Directed Lesson:

1. ***Establish the Need:*** Teacher initiates a discussion about the relevance and benefits of the skill. Completing assignments shows that you can work independently and be responsible. It is also important to complete assignments in order to be successful in school.

2. ***Introduction:*** The teacher will read the following story to the class:

    "It was Saturday morning and Sally was watching her favorite cartoon. Sally's mom had something she wanted Sally to do. When Sally's mom told her what she wanted Sally to do, Sally kept her eyes on the T.V. set. When Sally's mom asked, "Did you hear me?" Sally said, Yes, Mom. An hour later Sally's mom said, Did you pick up your toys yet? Sally said, I will Mom. An hour later, Sally's mom said angrily, Sally, I told you to pick up your toys! Sally said, O.K., O.K. Sally picked up some of her toys and then went outside to play."

Questions:	Did Sally listen to her mother?
	Did she finish the job her mom gave her?
	Do you think Sally could have done the job her mom gave her?
	Do you think you would do well in school if you didn't finish your work?
	Why do you think you should finish all your work?

3. ***Identify the Skill Components:*** (List on board before class)

    1. Listen to instructions and ask questions.
    2. Get materials out.
    3. Begin working.
    4. Keep working.
    5. Check your work.
    6. Finish your work neatly.

4. ***Model the Skill:*** Teacher reads the following letter to the class and acts it out: **"Dear (teacher's name), Will you please erase the writing on the board, clean out the pencil sharpener, and straighten the desk before you leave today. Thank you. The Custodian."**

5. *Behavioral Rehearsal:*

    A. *Selection:* The teacher will select four or more children to role play the following instructions.

    B. *Role Play:*

        1. Your mom has told you to clean your room. Your favorite T.V. program is on. What do you do?

        2. You are working on a paper at school. After awhile you feel like drawing a picture. What do you do?

        3. You are at home doing homework. You didn't listen to the directions, so you don't know how to do the paper. What do you do?

        4. The teacher is in the reading group. The person sitting next to you is acting silly. What do you do?

    C. *Completion:* After each role play, reinforce correct behavior, identify inappropriate behaviors, and reenact role play with corrections. If there are no corrections, role play is complete.

    D. *Reinforcers:* material rewards, verbal praise, self-praise, non-verbal reinforcements from teacher. Also, children who complete work neatly and on time can be given 5 minutes of additional free time.

    E. *Discussion:* Teacher asks children to discuss how well she completed her tasks for the custodian. Also discuss how well the children role played their situations. Would other children have handled it differently?

6. *Practice:* Students complete handwriting assignment in class as neatly as possible.

Give children copies of the following activity sheet, "Before and After Pictures." Ask them to draw a picture of Sally cleaning up her room, and a "before/after" picture of Sally's room.

7. *Independent Use:* Have children complete the school assignment at home.

8. *Continuation:* Teachers should remind children how important it is to complete school assignments as well as tasks assigned by adults at home. Being able to complete a job assigned to them shows that they are able to work independently, without having to be directed at every step by the teacher or other adult.

CHILDREN'S LITERATURE

Preller, James. *Wake Me in Spring.* New York: Scholastic, 1994.

Name _____   Date _____

BEFORE AND AFTER PICTURES

Directions: In Box A, draw a picture of Sally's room **before** she picked up some of her toys. Then in Box B, show Sally's room **after** she has picked up her toys.

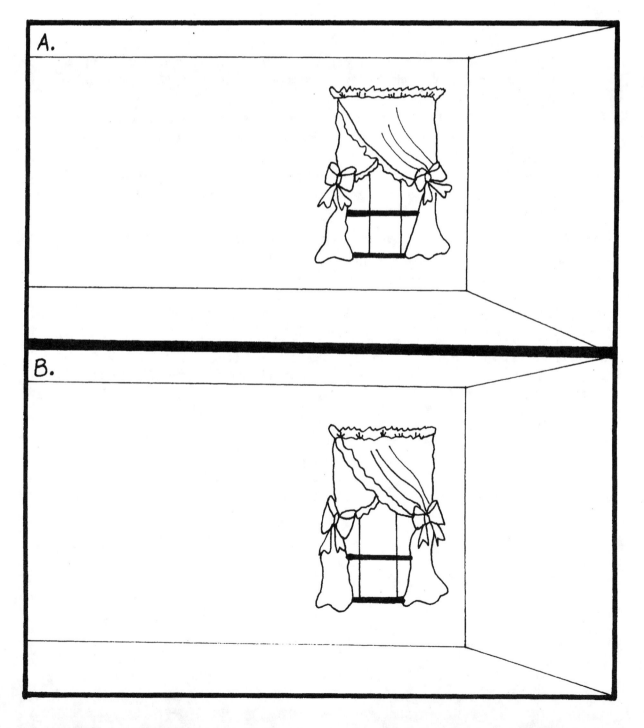

COMPLETING ASSIGNMENTS

Lesson 35

SOCIAL SKILL

Completing Assignments in a Given Time Period

Behavioral Objective: The learner will be able to neatly complete an assignment given by the teacher, or another adult, in a given amount of time.

Directed Lesson:

1. **Establish the Need:** Teacher reviews how completing assignments on time shows that the student is responsible and cares about the work. Completing assignments is also necessary in order to do well in school.

2. **Introduction:** The teacher will read the following poem to the class:

   > **Roses are red**
   > **Violets are blue**
   > **I have some work**
   > **That I must do.**
   >
   > **It has to be done**
   > **And after I do it**
   > **I then hand it in.**
   > **So know when to finish**
   > **And when to begin.**
   >
   > **I want to be neat**
   > **I won't work too fast**
   > **But I need to keep working**
   > **To finish the task.**
   >
   > **When the bell rings**
   > **Our work will be done**
   > **We'll all play a game**
   > **And laugh and have fun.**

   Teacher asks the children, **"What's the poem telling us?"** (First we work and then we play, finish what you start.)

3. **Identify the Skill Components:** (List on board before class)

   1. Listen to the directions and ask questions.
   2. Get materials out.
   3. Begin working.
   4. Keep working.

    5. Check your work.

    6. Make certain that your work is finished and neat.

4. ***Model the Skill:*** Teacher will role play a student in school. She will get out materials she knows she will need. (This may vary depending on the class.) She will sharpen her pencil. Next, she will begin her work, or any task that is applicable to what the class is doing. She completes the work neatly and quietly. (This can also be done on the board.)

5. ***Behavioral Rehearsal:***

    A. *Selection:* The teacher will select four students.

    B. *Role Play:* The teacher will individually give each student a task to do on the chalkboard in a given amount of time.

        Examples: 1. Write your first and last name.

                          2. Add these two numbers: $5 + 4 = $ _____

                          3. Write the numeral(s) that show today's date.

                          4. Draw a circle and a square shape.

    C. *Completion:* After each role play, reinforce correct behavior, identify inappropriate behaviors, and reenact role play with corrections. If there are no corrections, role play is complete.

    D. *Reinforcers:* material rewards, verbal praise (such as):

    "I like the way your pencil is out and ready."

    "I noticed that _____ kept working on the assignment until the time was up."

    "I am very pleased that _____ checked over his/her work when he/she was finished."

    "_____ completed the assignment and look how lovely it looks because it's neat."

    E. *Discussion:* Teacher reviews with the class the tasks completed by the role playing participants. Such questions as the following may be asked:

        1. Did each student listen to my directions?

        2. Did each student keep working?

        3. Did each student check his work?

        4. Was each student's work neat?

        5. Did each student finish his task?

6. ***Practice:*** Students will be asked to discuss any problems they have in completing work at school or at home, in a given amount of time.

7. ***Independent Use:*** Give children copies of the following activity sheet *Letter to Parent* and an   X   amount of time to complete it, as determined by the teacher.

8. ***Continuation:*** They can work with a partner. One can be the time keeper and one can do the task. Then, reverse the roles. After practicing this in class, children may be able to take the same assignment and practice at home.

CHILDREN'S LITERATURE

Carle, Eric. *The Very Hungry Caterpillar.* New York: Putnam Pub. (Animals) Group, 1981.

Singer, Marilyn. *Turtle in July.* New York: Macmillan Children's Group, 1989.

Name _____ Date _____

LETTER TO PARENT

Dear Parent,

I would like your child to spend _____ minutes on the following homework assignment. After this amount of time has gone by, please make a note of where the child is before it is completed, and then answer the questions at the bottom of this page. I would sincerely appreciate your cooperation.

Your Child's Teacher

Directions: Read and write each word.

1. dog   2. play

_____

_____

3. car   4. day

_____

_____

5. you   6. me

_____

_____

7. can   8. go

_____

_____

Questions for Parent   YES   NO

1. Did you child work steadily?   _____   _____

2. Did your child check his/her work?   _____   _____

3. Did your child finish his/her work on time? _____   _____

4. Did your child do a neat job?   _____   _____

Parents' Signature(s)   _____

_____

SOCIAL SKILL

Completing Assignments When You Make an Agreement

Behavioral Objective: The children will complete an assignment presented by the teacher.

Directed Lesson:

1. **Establish the Need:** Teacher begins a discussion about the relevance and benefits of the skill. Completing assignments is a necessary life-skill as well as a necessary academic skill. It is necessary to complete any goals that lead to success and self-confidence in various areas of a person's life.

2. **Introduction:** Teacher will say:

   "Pretend you are a house painter and you earn the money to support your family by painting houses. Each time you get ready to paint a house you must agree with the owner on the amount of money you will receive when the assignment has been completed. After you have completed only half the assignment, you stop to go fishing and to look for other jobs. How do you think the homeowner will feel? What do you think he might do? How do you think your family might feel? What do you think they will have to do? What should the house painter have done?"

3. **Identify the Skill Components:** (List on board before class)

   1. Learn to ask questions if you don't understand the directions.
   2. Learn to get the materials you need for the assignment.
   3. Begin work at once.
   4. Don't stop working.
   5. Complete the assignment.

4. **Model the Skill:** Teacher models the skill by coloring an umbrella previously drawn on the board.

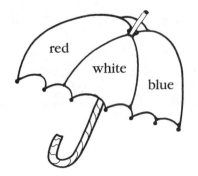

Directions:
Color each section of the umbrella using the color indicated.

5. **Behavioral Rehearsal:**

     A. *Selection:* Teacher selects pairs of children to role play various situations.

     B. *Role Play:* Teacher gives students role plays on cards previously prepared, such as: student-teacher (school assignment); parent-child (chores); employer-employee (work assignment); friend-friend (keeping a promise); sibling-sibling (completing chores).

     C. *Completion:* After each role play, reinforce correct behavior, identify inappropriate behaviors, and reenact role play with corrections. If there are no corrections, role play is complete.

     D. *Reinforcers:* material rewards, verbal praise, non-verbal expressions of approval (i.e., smile, pat, hug), and group reinforcement. If everyone completes a given task within a certain time frame, class will be rewarded with a story.

     E. *Discussion:* Have the children discuss the importance of completing jobs, assignments, games, books, and other activities. Discuss how it feels to complete a task. Ask the children what problems arise when they try to complete an assignment.

6. **Practice:** Give children copies of the following activity sheet, "Umbrella Scramble." The children will unscramble the six color words on the umbrella, print them on the correct line, and color the page. The answers are:

     1. purple
     2. green
     3. yellow
     4. orange
     5. red
     6. blue

7. **Independent Use:**

     A. Students bring a note from parents showing that they have completed their chores at home.

     B. Students complete all activities assigned by the teacher, and keep track on a daily chart.

8. **Continuation:** Teachers should point out the importance of completing any assignment we have agreed to, as related situations arise.

CHILDREN'S LITERATURE

Spier, Peter. *Peter Spier's Rain.* New York: Doubleday, 1987.

_____. *Noah's Ark.* New York: Dell, 1992.

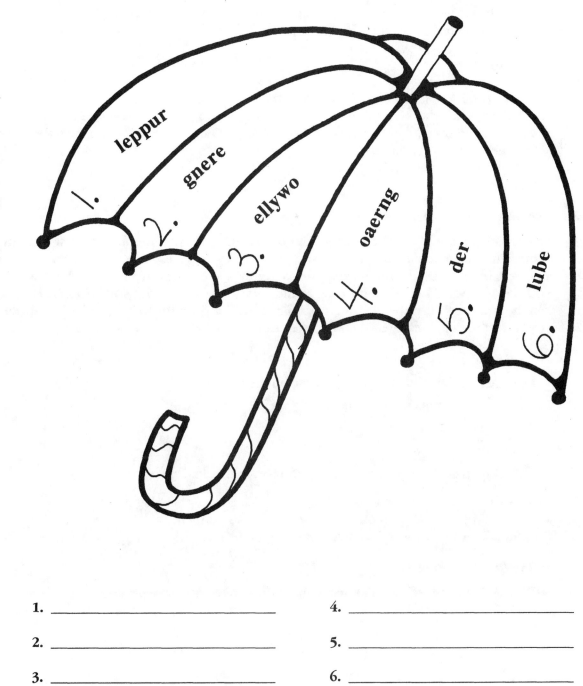

Name _____   Date _____

UMBRELLA SCRAMBLE

Don't let the six scrambled color words fool you. Unscramble
them and write them on the appropriate line below. Then color
the umbrella to show that you have solved the scramble.

leppur

gnere

ellywo

oaerng

der

lube

1.   _____

2.   _____

3.   _____

4.   _____

5.   _____

6.   _____

COMPLETING ASSIGNMENTS

SOCIAL SKILL

Completing Assignments Neatly and Accurately

Behavioral Objective: The children will complete an assignment presented by the teacher within a specified time limit.

Directed Lesson:

1. **Establish the Need:** Review with the class the concept that completing assignments leads to a feeling of success and self-confidence. Stress that it is important to feel proud of the work completed, and that it should be as neat as possible. Also stress the point that there are times when they will have a limited amount of time to finish a task. This occurs in the school, home, or work environment. They must learn how to pace themselves in order to work neatly and quickly.

2. **Introduction:** Teacher will say:

   "Suppose you are given a math test that has twenty-five problems and must be completed in twenty-five minutes! What do you think would happen if you worked very fast but made messy numbers that you knew were correct, but that the teacher could not read? What do you think would happen if you wrote your numerals very neatly, but only completed fifteen problems in the time limit? What would happen if you wrote very neatly and completed all the work?"

3. **Identify the Skill Components:** (List on board before class)

   1. Ask questions if you don't understand the directions.
   2. Get the materials you need for the assignment.
   3. Begin work at once.
   4. Don't stop working.
   5. Complete the assignment neatly and within the time allowed.

4. **Model the Skill:** Teacher models the skill by writing in her best handwriting: *I CAN COMPLETE ALL MY WORK NEATLY AND QUICKLY.* An assignment can be written on the board for the teacher to follow and must also include a time limit.

5. **Behavioral Rehearsal:**

   A. *Selection:* Teacher will select four pairs of children to role play.

B. *Role Play:* The pairs of children will work on puzzles, helping each other. They will be given a specific time to complete the puzzles neatly. Individual children may be selected to complete any assigned (short-term) projects in a specified time period (tidying up the library corner, picking up all floor scraps, cleaning the listening center area, straightening up the science table, etc.).

C. *Completion:* After each role play, reinforce correct behavior, identify inappropriate behaviors, and reenact role play with corrections. If there are no corrections, role play is complete.

D. *Reinforcers:* material rewards, verbal praise, and group reinforcement. When the classroom environment is neat and clean, turn out the lights and listen to a story record.

E. *Discussion:* Students will discuss the importance of being able to complete work neatly within a time limit.

6. ***Practice:*** Have the class complete the following math activity sheet, "I'm Getting Better and Better," *neatly* within five minutes. Or, have students write spelling words neatly within a given time period.

7. ***Independent Use:***

A. Students bring a note from parents stating that they completed assigned chores neatly within a time limit.

B. Students complete all activities assigned by the teacher neatly and within the time allotted.

8. ***Continuation:*** Teachers should remind children that completing tasks within the given time and as neatly as possible will help them be more successful in school.

CHILDREN'S LITERATURE

Hoban, Tana. *Twenty-Six Letters and Ninety-Nine Cents.* New York: Wm. Morrow (Greenwillow), 1987.

Name _____   Date _____

I'M GETTING BETTER AND BETTER

Directions: Add (+) or subtract (−) each problem. You will have five minutes to work. How many can you do?

1.   9
   −3
   ―――
	2. 6
	   +2
	   ―――
		3. 8
		   −0
		   ―――

4.   5
   +1
   ―――
	5. 3
	   +2
	   ―――
		6. 7
		   +2
		   ―――

7.   3
   +4
   ―――
	8. 4
	   +4
	   ―――
		9. 8
		   +1
		   ―――

10.   2
   +2
   ―――
	11. 3
	   −3
	   ―――
		12. 7
		   −0
		   ―――

13.   9
   −6
   ―――
	14. 1
	   +0
	   ―――
		15. 5
		   +3
		   ―――

Do this page again and again to increase your speed and accuracy.

SOCIAL SKILL

Completing Assignments for Success

Behavioral Objective: The children will work on an assigned task until it is finished.

Directed Lesson:

1. ***Establish the Need:*** Children need to know that completing a task is important for success in all areas. Feeling good about yourself and having pride in completing your work is the pay-off.

2. ***Introduction:*** Teacher writes this short paragraph on the board to be copied.

    "Waikiki Beach is the most famous beach in Hawaii. It offers excellent swimming, surfing lessons, canoe rides, and sun bathing."

    Ask children to find the main idea and supporting details. This helps us understand what we read. Each of us takes pride in completing an assignment correctly.

3. ***Identify the Skill Components:*** (List on board before class)

    1. Make sure you understand the task.

    2. Have materials ready.

    3. Work on task.

    4. Complete task.

4. ***Model the Skill:*** Teacher models skill steps by completing a short assignment on the board, such as "Put these three words in alphabetical order—sun, Hawaii, beach."

5. ***Behavioral Rehearsal:***

    A. *Selection:* Teacher selects five children to role play.

    B. *Role Play:*

    1. Student reads a designated paragraph in the reading book. Class helps to determine the main idea and supporting details.

    2. Student reads a paragraph in a science book. Class helps to determine the main idea and supporting details.

    3. Three children will complete tasks such as, erasing words from the board, handing out paper, and piling books on the shelf.

    C. *Completion:* After each role play, reinforce correct behavior, identify inappropriate behaviors, and reenact role play with corrections. If there are no corrections, role play is complete.

D. *Reinforcers:* Praise correct behavior verbally with comments like these:

1. **"You finished, Cindy. That's great!"**
2. **"Tony, your answer is right. Good work!"**
3. **"Ronique, you found the main idea. Let's write it on the chalkboard."**

E. *Discussion:* Talk with the children about why it's important to complete an assignment. Stress that completing assignments frees you up to do other interesting things and that completing assignments makes you feel good about the work you completed.

6. ***Practice:*** Give children copies of the following activity sheet, "Get Going, Droopy!" to complete.

7. ***Independent Use:***

A. Have children complete assigned written tasks at home and have parents sign them.

B. Every morning a few children can share information about these tasks.

8. ***Continuation:*** Teachers should remind children that completing assignments is important for success in school and in all areas of life.

CHILDREN'S LITERATURE

Snyder, Dianne. *The Boy of the Three-Year Nap.* Boston: Houghton Mifflin, 1993.

Name _____   Date _____

"GET GOING, DROOPY!"

Write a story about Droopy the Wonder Dog, who finally wakes up and gets his schoolwork done. When you have finished, underline the main idea in your story.

SOCIAL SKILL

Completing Assignments at Home

Behavioral Objective: The children will complete and return homework on time.

Directed Lesson:

1. ***Establish the Need:*** Teacher states that a need for practice is the reason for homework. Establish that completing tasks and practice are both necessary for success in school, at work, and in developing a feeling of self-worth. Discuss the consequences of not finishing the task. If you don't finish, people can't count on you. And if people can't count on you, then you don't have feelings of success and pride in what you do.

2. ***Introduction:*** Read this story about a child who finished homework and got enough practice to learn a skill:

   "Jane didn't know her multiplication facts. In order to learn them, she practiced each night. This became her homework assignment. Soon she knew them well enough to make an A on her fact test."

3. ***Identify the Skill Components:*** (List on board before class)

   1. Understand the assignment.
   2. Write down the assignment.
   3. Prepare materials.
   4. Complete and return homework.

4. ***Model the Skill:*** Teacher models the skill steps on the board using a short math homework assignment.

5. ***Behavioral Rehearsal:***

   A. *Selection:* Teacher selects three students to role play doing homework.

   B. *Role Play:* Role play each step in proper sequence.

   1. Understand the assignment (e.g., 25 math problems).
   2. Prepare the materials needed (paper, pencil, book).
   3. Take materials home.
   4. Find a quiet place to work.
   5. Ask for help if needed.
   6. Complete and return assignment.

C. *Completion:* After each role play, reinforce correct behavior, identify inappropriate behaviors, and reenact role play with corrections. If there are no corrections, role play is complete.

D. *Reinforcers:* Award a certificate for role playing and completing homework. Use verbal praise: "Smile, that's terrific! Good thinking." Also, children can make sets of math flashcards, one for home and one for school.

E. *Discussion:* Have children discuss role plays. Did Sue (role player) remember each step? What are the advantages of finishing homework? What problems have you had completing homework? How can you overcome these problems?

6. ***Practice:*** Give children copies of the following homework activity sheet, "Try for a Month of Smiles," and have them keep a record of their homework using the face symbols on the chart. Make a folder for keeping the homework activity sheets for the year.

7. ***Independent Use:***

A. Use a homework activity sheet to record *completed* homework.

B. Have the parents sign completed homework every night.

8. ***Continuation:*** Teachers will remind children of the purpose of homework assignments—"practice makes perfect."

CHILDREN'S LITERATURE

Byars, Betsy. *Go and Hush the Baby.* New York: Puffin Books, 1982.

Giff, Patricia Reilly. *Today Was a Terrible Day.* New York: Viking Children's Books, 1984.

Name _____

Month _____

TRY FOR A MONTH OF SMILES

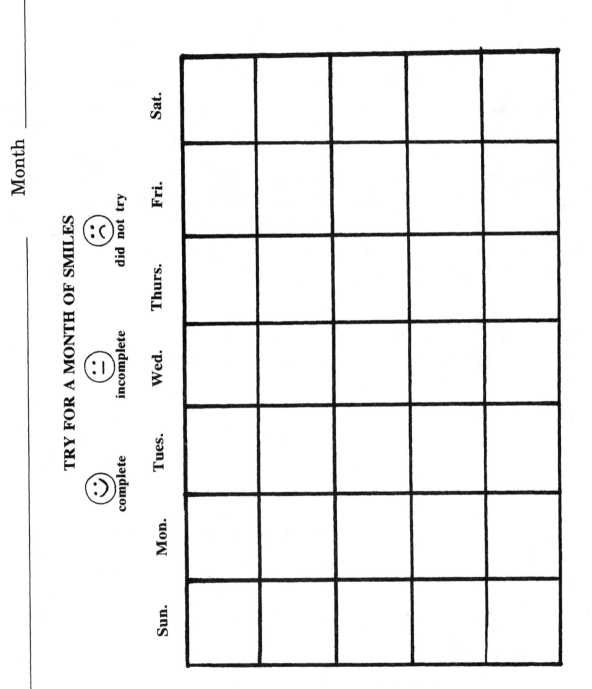

😊 complete   😐 incomplete   ☹ did not try

Sun.	Mon.	Tues.	Wed.	Thurs.	Fri.	Sat.

SOCIAL SKILL

Expressing Your Own Anger (Mitzy & Fritzy I)

Behavioral Objective: The children will communicate anger by use of nonthreatening words and actions.

Directed Lesson:

1. **Establish the Need:** Teacher will initiate a discussion of the relevance and benefits of the skill. Maintaining self-control and communicating anger by use of nonthreatening words and actions will most likely prevent an escalation of the problem from a verbal to a physical level. Fighting does not solve the problem. Only communication and compromise can achieve that.

2. **Introduction:** Teacher will read the following story to the class.

   Materials: Mitzy & Fritzy puppets (see pattern on page 134)

   2 popsicle sticks

   Teacher will read the following story using both puppets.

   Fritzy and Mitzy were walking home from the carnival, each carrying a balloon they bought with their allowance. All of a sudden Fritzy looked up and said, "Oh no! I accidentally let go of my balloon!" (He tried to reach up and grab it). "Come back here! I want my balloon!" (Fritzy turned to Mitzy) He said, "That's not fair! You have a balloon and I don't!" Mitzy said, "Sorry Fritzy, but you let go of yours and I didn't." (Fritzy takes a deep breath) He said to Mitzy, "I know Mitzy but I'm angry that it happened to me." "What are you going to do now?" asked Mitzy. "Well, I guess I'll have to wait until I get my allowance again. Then I'll buy another one," said Fritzy. "Until then," said Mitzy "We can both play with my balloon."

   Teacher will ask the students the following questions:

   ▸ **Why was Fritzy angry?**

   ▸ **What would you have done if you were Fritzy?**

   ▸ **What did Fritzy do?**

   ▸ **Did he do the right thing when he got mad? Why? Why not?**

   ▸ **How was his problem solved?**

3. **Identify the Skill Components:** (List on board before class)

   1. When you are angry with yourself, stop and breathe deeply.

   2. Analyze your feelings.

   3. Decide why you feel this way.

4. Decide what to do to stop your angry feeling.

5. Decide how to act.

6. Select a good way to show your anger and get rid of it.

4. **Model the Skill:** The teacher will model the skill steps by expressing displeasure with him/herself. She will tell the children in a non-aggressive manner that she is upset at him/herself because he/she was careless and spilled water on the floor. Stress to the class that a person must use self-control at all times. Stress that the anger is always directed at the behavior or act and not at a person.

5. **Behavioral Rehearsal:**

A. *Selection:* The teacher will select four students to role play.

B. *Role Play:*

1. *Teacher/Student:* The teacher is ready to collect the morning work. You are not finished. What do you do?

2. *Teacher/Student:* The teacher hears noises across the room. She sees the student next to you talking and thinks you were talking too. You know you were not. What do you do?

3. *Teacher/Student:* The class is going on a field trip to the zoo. You forgot to return your permission slip. The teacher says you can't go. What do you do?

4. *Student/Student:* You and another student are the only two left in the math game. The other student answers the problem _____ + _____ = _____ first. He/she is the winner. What do you do?

C. *Completion:* After each role play, reinforce correct behavior, identify inappropriate behaviors, and reenact role play with corrections. If there are no corrections, role play is complete.

D. *Reinforcers:* Acknowledge correct behavior with material rewards and verbal praise like the following:

   "I noticed how _____ took a deep breath before reacting."

   "I liked the way _____ talked about his anger without hitting."

   "_____ did you choose not to act out because you thought about what might happen to you both if you did?"

   "I could tell that _____ had self-control because he did _____ instead of acting out."

E. *Discussion:* Afterwards, discuss whether the action the angry student chose to take was right or wrong. Also discuss alternative actions in handling the situation.

6. **Practice:** Give children copies of the following activity sheet, "Taking Turns," to complete and check in class.

7. **Independent Use:**

A. The teacher will distribute a sheet of paper to each student. He/she will say, **"Tonight when you get home from school, your parents might tell you to do** something you don't feel like doing such as your homework, or washing dishes, or turning off the T.V. or going to bed early. I want you to either write a story or draw a picture of something that made you angry at home. Show how you acted when you got angry."

B. Discuss the stories in class.

8. *Continuation:* Teachers should stress the importance of communicating anger in non-threatening words and actions, as related situations arise.

CHILDREN'S LITERATURE

Sharmat, Marjorie Weinman. *Attila the Angry.*

Udry, Janice May. *Let's Be Enemies.* New York: Harper Collins Children's Books, 1988.

STICK PUPPETS

Fritzy

Mitzy

Name _____   Date _____

TAKING TURNS

Read the paragraph below. Choose the correct word from the **WORD BANK** to complete each sentence, and write it on the line. Then read the paragraph again.

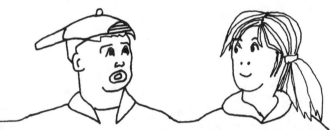

Jim said, "I want a turn on the slide. I think I will _____ into the line." "You _____ do that," said Sara. Jim _____ about what Sara said. He was _____ but he did not want to get in trouble. "OK," he said, "I'll _____ something else to do." Jim ran away from Sara and _____ tag with Beth and Ken.

WORD BANK

| played | mad | thought | cut | find | can't |

SOCIAL SKILL

Handling Another Persons' Anger (Mitzy & Fritzy II)

Behavioral Objective: The children will deal with another person's anger by helping to resolve the conflict using nonthreatening words and actions.

Directed Lesson:

1. **Establish the Need:** Teacher will initiate a discussion about the relevance and benefits of the skill. If one person tries to resolve a conflict in a nonthreatening manner, the other person will usually agree and the conflict will be more easily settled. Communication solves problems and fighting creates more problems.

2. **Introduction:** Teacher reads the following story using the Fritzy and Mitzy puppets from the previous lesson.

    Mitzy and Fritzy were lining up for lunch. Mitzy turned around angrily and said, "Did you step on my shoe?" Fritzy said, "Yes, but I didn't mean to—it was an accident." As they walked down the hall to lunch the same thing happened again. This time Mitzy was *really* angry. So she turned around and said, "Fritzy, cut it out!" Fritzy got angry because Mitzy yelled at him in front of the other kids and so he wanted to yell back at Mitzy. Then he thought about what Mitzy had said and why she was angry. He knows he would be mad if someone kept stepping on the back of *his* shoe. So instead of yelling back or hitting Mitzy, he said, "You're right Mitzy, I'm sorry." "I should really watch where I am going."

    Teacher will ask the children the following questions:

    ❥ **Why was Mitzy mad at Fritzy?**
    ❥ **Would you be mad at Fritzy?**
    ❥ **What did Mitzy do with her anger?**
    ❥ **What did Fritzy do with his anger?**
    ❥ **Did either Fritzy or Mitzy get into trouble? Why not?**

3. **Identify the Skill Components:** (List on board before class.)

    1. Listen to the other person.
    2. Tell your story.
    3. Think about how you both feel.
    4. Decide what will happen if a fight starts.
    5. Decide what is the right thing to do.
    6. Decide what you should do.

136

4. ***Model the Skill:*** The teacher will model the skill steps by showing what she would do if someone was angry with her. Ask a child to pretend that he/she is angry at the teacher for not letting him/her pass out papers.

5. ***Behavioral Rehearsal:***

   A. *Selection:* The teacher will select four pairs of children to role play. The teacher will read each role play situation aloud.

   B. *Role Play:*

      1. *Student/Student:* You and a friend are playing tag on the playground. You tag your friend and accidentally knock him/her down. He/she gets angry. What do you do?

      2. *Student/Student:* You are working at your desk. You see a pencil on the floor. You pick it up and keep it. A classmate comes up to you and says it is his/hers. He/she tries to grab it from you. What do you do?

      3. *Student/Student:* You and a friend are telling jokes at lunch. Your friend just got a haircut so you decide to tease him/her about it. He/she gets angry. What do you do?

      4. *Teacher/Student:* The teacher sees you throw a wad of paper in class. She makes you sit in the time-out chair. A few minutes later she sees you writing on the desk. She tells you she will have to call your parents. You get scared and angry because you know you will get into trouble at home. What do you do?

   C. *Completion:* After each role play, reinforce correct behavior, identify inappropriate behaviors, and reenact role play with corrections. If there are no corrections, role play is complete.

   D. *Reinforcers:* Praise correct behavior verbally, for example:

      "_____ **did a very good job of controlling your anger without hitting.**"

      "**I like the way _____ listened to what happened before reacting.**"

      "_____ **you really showed great self-control by not _____.**"

      "**I noticed how _____ really tried to talk over the problem.**"

      "_____ **you really thought of a good way to solve the problem so that neither of you would get in trouble.**"

   E. *Discussion:* A discussion of whether the action the angry student chose to take was right or wrong, and also the advantages of peaceful negotiation.

6. ***Practice:*** Using the following activity sheet, *What Did I Do? How Can I Fit It?* the children will be asked to think about a time when someone in their family or a friend was angry with them. Ask yourself, "What did I do?" and "How can I fix it?"

7. ***Independent Use:***

   A. Have students write and/or draw their parents, brothers, sisters, or any relative that might be angry with them and have them state what they did do wrong. Have the person who was angry sign the paper.

   B. Discuss the stories in school and devise other or better methods of handling another person's anger.

8. **Continuation:** Teachers should continue to remind children that it usually pays to try to resolve a problem peacefully.

CHILDREN'S LITERATURE

Anderson, Peggy Perry. *Wendle, What Have You Done?* Boston: Houghton Mifflin, 1994.

Lexau, Joan M. *Trouble Will Find You.* Boston: Hougton Mifflin, 1994.

Name _____   Date _____

WHAT DID I DO? HOW CAN I FIX IT?

Directions: Use your crayons and in each square make a picture to illustrate the sentence.

OH! OH! ONE DAY THIS HAPPENED!

THIS IS WHAT I DID TO HELP THE SITUATION.

SOCIAL SKILL
Using Nonthreatening Words

Behavioral Objective: The children will deal with another person's anger by helping to resolve the conflict using nonthreatening words and actions.

Directed Lesson:

1. **Establish the Need:** Teacher reviews the importance of using nonthreatening words and actions to resolve any conflict. Also explain that dealing with someone else's anger is different from handling your own. Both can be dealt with in a similar fashion and both are important in order to prevent fights.

2. **Introduction:** Teacher presents the following situation to the class: **"Suppose the class is playing a game such as 'Doggie, Doggie, Where's Your Bone?' One person is chosen to be the 'Doggie' and the other one hides the 'Bone.' You become excited and yell out where the bone is. The person who is looking for it becomes very angry and says that you cheated and ruined the game. You know that someone is very angry with you. How do you think you would feel? What do you think you could do to prevent a fight? How do you think your actions would affect the other person? What will you do different the next time?"**

3. **Identify the Skill Components:** (List on board before class.)

   1. Listen to the other person.
   2. Think about how that person feels.
   3. Think about what will happen if you use threatening words.
   4. Talk to the person with nonthreatening words.
   5. Try to solve the problem with words rather than actions.

4. **Model the Skill:** Teacher models the behavior by responding with nonthreatening words to an angry student. The student may be angry about anything he can think of that could happen in the school setting.

5. **Behavioral Rehearsal:**

   A. *Selection:* Teacher selects four pairs of children to role play.

   B. *Role Play:* Students role play situations in which they must respond appropriately to another's anger. You can either give them the role plays, or they may make up their own role plays.

C. *Completion:* After each role play, reinforce correct behavior, identify inappropriate behaviors, and reenact role play with corrections. If there are no corrections, role play is complete.

D. *Reinforcers:* Reinforce the appropriate reactions to another's anger. Praise them or give non-verbal praise such as a handshake, smile, and pat on the back. Other children should praise any appropriate response.

E. *Discussion:* Discuss the importance of using self-control when someone is angry at you by not getting them angrier. By using nonthreatening words, it gives the other person a chance to listen and perhaps change his/her mind. Discuss the difficulties that may emerge when dealing with someone's anger.

6. ***Practice:*** Have children complete the following worksheet, "Words to Ease Anger." Children will list words that can be used to ease angry feelings. Then they select the ones they like best to write on the tail of the kite.

7. ***Independent Use:***

A. Each morning discuss any situations that may have happened on the way to school that called for a child to handle someone's anger.

B. Students will respond appropriately to anger of other students during all school activities. These incidents should be kept in individual diaries.

8. ***Continuation:*** Teachers should continue to encourage children to use nonthreatening words in response to another's anger.

CHILDREN'S LITERATURE

Gantos, Jack. *Not So Rotten Ralph.* Boston: Houghton Mifflin, 1994.

Name _____   Date _____

WORDS TO EASE ANGER

Directions: Suppose someone is angry! Think of some soothing words that YOU could say to help others control their anger. Your teacher will write these words on the chalkboard.

       Choose **THREE** words. Write one on each kite tail. Decorate the kite.

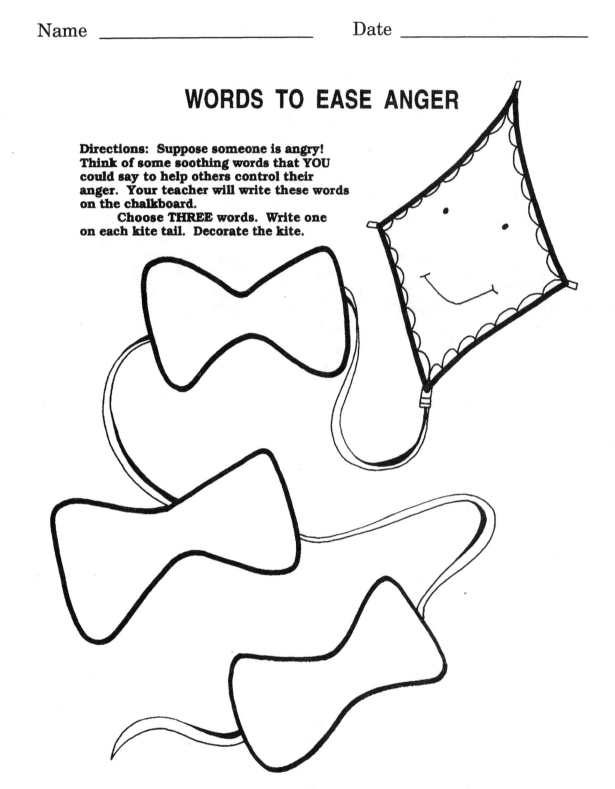

SOCIAL SKILL

Expressing Feelings

Behavioral Objective: Children will identify feelings and express them verbally.

Directed Lesson:

1. **Establish the Need:** Teacher initiates a discussion about how expressing feelings will help you deal with your feelings.

2. **Introduction:** Teacher will have class discussions about feelings. Teacher will ask what are the reasons for feeling happy, sad, angry, etc. What are the advantages of telling others how we feel?

3. **Identify the Skill Components:** Write the following skill components on the board or on sentence strips.

    1. Think how you feel.
    2. Plan what to say.
    3. Raise your hand.
    4. Wait to be called on.
    5. Express your feelings.

4. **Model the Skill:** Select a student to ask the teacher how she/he feels when everyone is ready to begin work. Teacher will reply.

5. **Behavioral Rehearsal:**

    A. *Selection:* Teacher will select four students to role play.

    B. *Role Play:* Have students express how they feel in one of the following situations:

        1. When you get 100% on a spelling test
        2. When you forget your homework
        3. When it is your birthday
        4. When you are sick

    C. *Completion:* After each role play, reinforce correct behavior, identify inappropriate behaviors, and reenact role play with corrections. If there are no corrections, role play is complete.

    D. *Reinforcers:* verbal encouragement, tangible rewards, smile. Set up a "Feeling Good" jar and have compliments written on tiny round shapes. When someone deserves a compliment, they can reach into the jar and read their good fortune. (*Examples:* "You are a Winner!" "You are nice." "What a great sport you are!" etc...)

    E. *Discussion:* Students discuss the role plays and corrections made. Teacher asks class what the advantages are to expressing feelings. (It makes you feel connected to others and not isolated.)

6.   *Practice:* Give children copies of the following activity sheet, "Expressing Feelings," to complete in class. Worksheet directions are to complete sentences, expressing the reason for the feeling.

7.   *Independent Use:*

    1. Students will be encouraged to express positive feelings outside of school to family members, friends, and adults.

    2. Teacher will ask children during bellwork time or other flexible time to share their feelings with the class and ask with whom they have enjoyed sharing their feelings with outside of class.

8.   *Continuation:* Teacher should encourage children to express positive feelings to others whenever they can. Sharing such feelings will please others as well as themselves.

CHILDREN'S LITERATURE

Simon, Norma. *How Do I Feel?* Morton Grove, IL: A. Whitman, 1970.

_____. *I Was So Mad!* Morton Grove, IL: A. Whitman, 1974.

Name _____   Date _____

EXPRESSING FEELINGS

1. I sometimes worry about _____

2. I get excited when _____

3. I feel important when_____

This is me doing what I like to do best.

I like to hear people say to me: " _____

_____ "

SOCIAL SKILL
Expressing Feelings (Mixed Emotions)

Behavioral Objective: Students verbally express how they feel and the reasons why.

Directed Lesson:

1. **Establish the Need:** Teacher will tell students that if we think about what caused our feelings, we can try to avoid unpleasant feelings. Also, if it was a happy feeling, we can look forward to that activity again. Why is it important to express feelings? (To feel connected and not isolated from others and to make others feel wanted and yourself to feel good.)

2. **Introduction:** Today we will complete the following sentences on the board.

    1. I feel scared when…
    2. I felt embarrassed when…
    3. I felt sad when…
    4. I am happy when…
    5. I get excited when…
    6. I feel proud when…
    7. I feel good when…

3. **Identify the Skill Components:** Write the following skill components on the board or on sentence strips.

    1. Think how you feel and why.
    2. Put your thoughts in a sentence.
    3. Wait to be called on.
    4. Express your feelings verbally.

4. **Model the Skill:** Teacher will express a happy feeling. The situation that called for the feeling was a birthday present.

5. **Behavioral Rehearsal:**

    A. *Selection:* Teacher will select three students to role play.

    B. *Role Play:* Children will express how they feel and why in regard to one of the situations below.

        1. Your friend broke your new CD player.
        2. Mother bought you a new school outfit.
        3. The field trip is cancelled.

146

    C. *Completion:* After each role play, reinforce correct behavior, identify inappropriate behaviors, and reenact role play with corrections. If there are no corrections, role play is complete.

    D. *Reinforcers:* verbal encouragement, tangible rewards, smile. Make a "Happy/Sad" wheel that children can spin. If it falls on "Happy," tell something that makes them feel happy, etc...

    E. *Discussion:* Students discuss the information they wrote in the "Introduction" section.

6. Practice: Have children complete the following activity sheet, "Synonym Circles," in which they are to match each circled word with a synonym taken from the wordbank.

7. Independent Use:

1. Students may write in a journal at home and then share their journals with the class or privately with the teacher.

2. Teacher will encourage students to express themselves and provide regular time to listen.

8. Continuation: Teacher should remind children that expressing our feelings to others is one important way to share our experiences.

CHILDREN'S LITERATURE

Henkes, Kevin. *Julius, the Baby of the World.* New York: Greenwillow, 1990.

Stanton, Elizabeth and Henry. *Sometimes I Like to Cry.* Morton Grove, IL: A. Whitman, 1978.

Name _____   Date _____

SYNONYM CIRCLES

<u>DO YOU KNOW WHAT SYNONYMS ARE?</u> They are two words that mean **almost** the same thing. Read the words in the WORDBANK. Write one next to its twin word in the synonym circle.

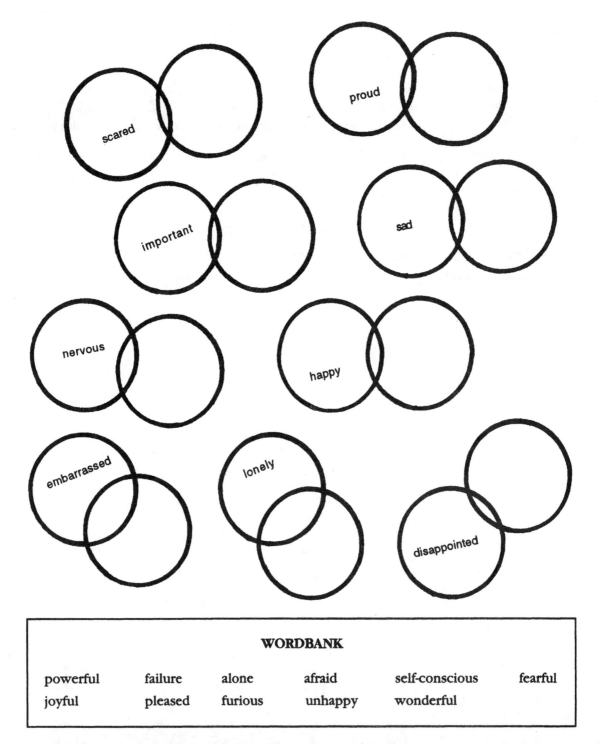

WORDBANK					
powerful	failure	alone	afraid	self-conscious	fearful
joyful	pleased	furious	unhappy	wonderful	

SOCIAL SKILL

Understanding the Need to Accept Change

Behavioral Objective: Children will be able to understand the need to accept necessary changes whether it makes them feel good or bad. When the students learn to accept changes, it will help to prepare them for a better life in the future.

Directed Lesson:

1. **Establish the Need:** Change is often difficult to accept, but is unavoidable in life. Like feelings, change can make one either happy or sad. It is necessary to accept changes that make one sad and to learn to create better situations in the future to acquire happiness.

2. **Introduction:** The teacher will say to the class:

   "Today we will not have _____." (Insert a particular class or lesson that is always given on this day.) "There has been a change in our schedule. How do you feel about that?" Children will respond. The teacher then asks, "do we have any control over this situation?" (Discussion with class.) "Can this become a good situation? How can we make this a good situation? How can we make the most of this change in our schedule?"

3. **Identify the Skill Components:** Write the following skill components on the board or on sentence strips.

   1. Identify changes you have experienced.
   2. Identify changes you can control and accept.
   3. Identify changes you cannot control.
   4. Learn to accept and/or control changes you cannot control.
   5. Learn appropriate reaction to change.

4. **Model the Skill:** Teacher will demonstrate the inappropriate reaction to a change in a student's day and the appropriate reaction to that same change. *Example:* Student was planning to play with a game during indoor recess and discovered that someone had already checked it out. Show negative and positive reaction to this situation (negative - holler, scream kick the chair, slam the door; positive - change to a different game, ask if you may join the game, try some activity you have not done before).

5. **Behavioral Rehearsal:**

   A. *Selection:* Teacher will choose students to role play.

149

B. *Role Play:* Children will role play their own reactions to changes they have experienced.

C. *Completion:* After each role play, reinforce correct behavior, identify inappropriate behaviors, and reenact role play with corrections. If there are no corrections, role play is complete.

D. *Reinforcers:* Give verbal praise to those children who follow skill components.

E. *Discussion:* Discuss difficulties in accepting change with appropriate reactions.

6. *Practice:* Give students copies of the following activity sheet, "All Aboard the Change Train." Children will draw a picture of a change they experienced in class and how they felt and reacted about that change *then,* when it occurred, and how they feel *now,* after that change was initiated.

7. *Independent Use:* Send another copy of the activity sheet home for the children to draw a picture of a change that took place at home and to indicate how they felt and reacted *then,* when it occurred, and how they feel *now.*

8. *Continuation:* Talk about the changes that took place at home. The teacher reminds children that this social skill usage will benefit them in social and academic relationships. By understanding and accepting changes and reacting appropriately to change, they will experience more happiness in life.

CHILDREN'S LITERATURE

Girard, Linda Walvoord. *We Adopted You, Benjamin Koo.* Morton Grove, IL: A. Whitman, 1989.

Henriod, Lorraine. *Grandma's Wheelchair.* Morton Grove, IL: A. Whitman, 1982.

Name _____   Date _____

ALL ABOARD! ALL ABOARD THE CHANGE TRAIN

What change happened to me today?

I will show you!

HOW DID IT MAKE ME FEEL?

THEN

NOW

Parent Comments: _____

_____

_____

Parent Signature _____

ACCEPTING CHANGE

SOCIAL SKILL

Accepting and Adjusting to Change

Behavioral Objective: Children will try to understand and accept change. This is necessary to learn to have a happy adult life.

Directed Lesson:

1. **Establish the Need:** Teacher reviews the benefits and relevance of the skill. Students need to accept change in order to alleviate stress in various situations. Not having this skill leads to over-reaction.

2. **Introduction:** The teacher will introduce the skill by saying, **"Gym has been cancelled this week."** Observe, then discuss class reaction. How is everyone feeling? Why did they react this way? What should we do now?

3. **Identify the Skill Components:** Write the following skill components on the board or on sentence strips.

    1. Learn that change cannot be avoided.
    2. Learn to accept change without complaint.
    3. Decide what is good and bad about the change.
    4. Adjust to change.

4. **Model the Skill:** Teacher models the skill by moving the children to different seats. She explains, **"The reason for changing seats is for you to get to know other students in your class."**

5. **Behavioral Rehearsal:**

    A. *Selection:* Teacher will select twelve students to role play various activities.

    B. *Role Play:* Discuss the idea that different people react differently to situations, and there is usually a reason why people pick a particular solution. Distribute a "What If" list and discuss choices children can make. After discussing all examples, have pairs of children act out the alternative behaviors.

    C. *Completion:* After each role play, reinforce correct behavior, identify inappropriate behaviors, and reenact role play with corrections. If there are no corrections, role play is complete.

    D. *Reinforcers:* verbal encouragement, group reinforcement and non-verbal expressions of approval.

    E. *Discussion:* Have children discuss the role plays and any inappropriate behaviors that need correction.

6. **Practice:** Students will complete the following "What If. . ." activity sheet by answering the questions.

7. **Independent Use:** Students will take the second activity sheet, "Teddy's Reaction to Changes," home to draw pictures.

    1. Learner reacts calmly when a change occurs and accepts it graciously.

    2. Learner relates incidents of change at home and his/her reaction to those changes.

8. **Continuation:** Teacher should remind children that being able to accept change is necessary to be happy. Life is full of changes and each of us must learn to adjust to them.

CHILDREN'S LITERATURE

Emmert, Michelle. *I'm the Big Dieter Now.* Morton Grove, IL: A Whitman, 1989.

Girard, Linda Walvoord. *At Daddy's on Saturdays.* Morton Grove, IL: A. Whitman, 1987.

Name _____   Date _____

WHAT IF...

Directions: How do you think Perry Parrot would feel if these things happened to him? Write your response on the lines below:

1. What if your class was going on a field trip and the bus didn't come?

   _____

   _____

2. What if your teacher is absent and you have a substitute?

   _____

   _____

3. What if gym was cancelled for the day?

   _____

   _____

4. What if it was raining and outdoor recess was cancelled?

   _____

   _____

5. What if one day your teacher cancelled spelling and gave you a party instead because of good behavior?

   _____

   _____

Name _____   Date _____

TEDDY'S REACTION TO CHANGES

This Teddy Bear has feelings, just like you do. Tell how he feels and reacts in the following situations:

The teacher changed his seat. Now he no longer sits next to his best friend.

A new bear comes into the classroom who looks different.

SOCIAL SKILL
Learning to Accept Change

Behavioral Objective: The children will discuss changes, and the importance of accepting them.

Directed Lesson:

1. **Establish the Need:** Teacher initiates discussion with class by stating: **"Everything changes, nothing stays the same. It's important to learn to accept the changes that occur."**

2. **Introduction:** Teacher asks the following questions:

   How have you changed since you were a baby?

   What are some of the changes that have happened to you that made you feel happy? (sad?)

   In what way is this year's class different from your class last year?

   How do these changes make you feel? Is there anything you can do about these changes?

3. **Identify the Skill Components:** (List on board or write on sentence strips)

   1. Think about the change.
   2. Identify your feelings about it.
   3. Learn to accept change without complaint.
   4. Learn to deal with the change.
   5. Learn to like the change.

4. **Model the Skill:** Teacher will model the skill by reading the following story. Afterwards, teacher will show the students the steps to follow.

   ### Camping Trip

   "The class was scheduled to go on a camping trip for three days. The students and their teacher spent weeks preparing for the trip. The day finally came. During the night before, there was a severe winter storm. When the students came to school the next day all packed and ready to go, they were told by their teacher that the trip had to be cancelled due to bad weather."

5. **Behavioral Rehearsal:**

   A. *Selection:* Teacher reads each situation and then chooses a student to follow the skills steps.

B. *Role Play: Situation 1* - "**Today the class was scheduled for gym. The children were quite excited because there was going to be a contest. After attendance had been taken, the teacher announced that there would be no gym today because the gym teacher was absent.**"

Situation 2—"**Saturday, Mark's family was planning to go to the zoo. That morning, Mark's mother received a phone call that Grandma was sick and needed her to take her to the hospital. Mother told Mark that the zoo trip had to be postponed.**"

C. *Completion:* After each role play, reinforce correct behaviors. Identify inappropriate behaviors, and reenact role play with corrections. If there are no corrections, role play is complete.

D. *Reinforcers:* Verbal praise - "**You did that well.**" "**You certainly followed the steps.**" Smile and nod head to show approval.

E. *Discussion:* Have students discuss role playing, and the corrections that were made. Ask the class why it is important to be able to accept change.

6. ***Practice:*** Give children copies of the following open-ended story, "A Change of Plans." Read through the story with the class and have students complete it. Afterwards, share responses.

7. ***Independent Use:*** Have students take home the record sheet "Changes at Home" and list weekly changes that the family might have experienced. They should return their record to class for a sharing session.

8. ***Continuation:*** Teachers tell students, "**If you use this skill whenever and wherever you need it you will feel better, and go on with your activities with a more positive outlook.**"

CHILDREN'S LITERATURE

Simon, Norma. *All Kinds of Families.* Morton Grove, IL: A Whitman, 1976.

Vigna, Judith. *Black Like Kyra, White Like Me.* Morton Grove, IL: A. Whitman, 1992.

Name _____   Date _____

A CHANGE OF PLANS

Directions: Complete the story.

     Sally and her mother made plans to go to the amusement park. Sally was excited all week. Early Saturday morning the phone rang. She was told that her Grandmother was ill and needed her mother to take her to the hospital.

_____

_____

_____

_____

_____

_____

_____

_____

_____

_____

_____

_____

_____

_____

_____

_____

Name _____   Date _____

CHANGES AT HOME

Directions: Make a list of changes that occur from Monday to Thursday in your home and how members of your family reacted to the changes. Return the worksheet on Friday to share with the class.

DAYS	CHANGES	REACTIONS
Mon.		
Tues.		
Wed.		
Thu.		
Fri.	Sharing Changes and Reactions	

SOCIAL SKILL
Recognizing False Accusations and Rumors

Behavioral Objective: The children will recognize false accusations and rumors and develop strategies to stop them.

Directed Lesson:

1. **Establish the Need:** The purpose is to console the person who is damaged by false rumors, and to recognize the need to not engage in spreading rumors.

2. **Introduction:** "Boys and girls, have you ever been blamed for something you did not do? How did it make you feel? Listen to the story of Ronnie and Reggie.

    "Ronnie and Reggie were best friends. They sat next to each other in class. One day, Ronnie could not find his pencils. He raised his hand and told the teacher that Reggie had taken his pencils. Everyone turned and looked at Reggie. Reggie began to cry. The teacher came over and questioned Reggie. Reggie denied taking Ronnie's pencils—after all they were best friends. The teacher had Ronnie look again very carefully, and sure enough, there under his reading book were the pencils."

    Teacher asks class:

    1. **Why was Reggie crying?**
    2. **How can a rumor affect others?**

3. **Identify the Skill Components:** (List on board before class or on sentence strips)

    1. Identify a rumor.
    2. Avoid starting a rumor.
    3. Avoid listening to rumors.
    4. Try to stop a rumor.

4. **Model the Skill:** Teacher models the skill by stating a rumor she heard and chose to ignore. In addition, she will avoid telling others the rumor.

5. **Behavioral Rehearsal:**

    A. *Selection:* Teacher selects children to role play. Children are chosen in groups of three.

    B. *Role Play:* One child tells a rumor, the second child demonstrates how to ignore a rumor by not passing it on to the third student.

160

C. *Completion:* After each role play, reinforce correct behavior, identify inappropriate behaviors, and reenact role play with corrections. If there are no corrections, role play is complete.

D. *Reinforcers:* material rewards, verbal praise, group reinforcement.

E. *Discussion:* Have children discuss role plays. A discussion will follow as to the correctness of the role play following each group of 3.

6. **Practice:** Distribute copies of the accompanying *Word Search* activity sheet for children to decipher by finding the hidden message relating to this lesson.

7. **Independent Use:**

A. Give children copies of the following activity sheet, "The Story of Ronnie and Reggie," for homework. Review the worksheet with children.

B. Answer questions from the homework sheet.

8. **Continuation:** Teacher should point out the need for continued use of this skill as similar situations arise.

CHILDREN'S LITERATURE

Wild Margaret. *All the Better to See You With!* Morton Grove, IL: A. Whitman, 1993.

Name_____   Date _____

WORD SEARCH

Find these hidden words:

| A | TELLING | AVOID | RUMOR |

```
A V O I D Z F G K

X T T E L L I N G

M P B C A N P B S

V Y W O R U M O R
```

NOW, write the hidden message:

_ _ _ _ _   _ _ _ _ _ _ _   _   _ _ _ _ _.

Parent Comments: _____

_____

_____

Parent Signature:_____

Name _____ Date _____

THE STORY OF RONNIE AND REGGIE

Ronnie and Reggie were best friends. They sat next to each other in class. One day, Ronnie could not find his pencils. He raised his hand and told the teacher that Reggie had taken his pencils. Everyone turned and looked at Reggie. Reggie began to cry. The teacher came over and questioned Reggie. Reggie denied taking Ronnie's pencils—after all, they were best friends. The teacher had Ronnie look again very carefully, and sure enough, there under his reading book were his pencils.

Write the letter for the answer on the line.

1. Who started the rumor? ____
2. How did Reggie feel? ____
3. What was the rumor about? ____

A. glad

B. missing pencils

C. sad

D. Reggie

E. missing crayons

F. Ronnie

Parent's Signature:

_____

Comments:

SOCIAL SKILL
Preventing False Rumors

Behavioral Objective: The children will be able to recognize rumors and develop strategies to stop them.

Directed Lesson:

1. ***Establish the Need:*** The teacher initiates a discussion about the relevance and consequences of false rumors. It is important for people to tell the truth if they want others to believe them. By starting or repeating false rumors, people can be hurt.

2. ***Introduction:*** The teacher asks the following questions: **"Have you heard a false rumor?" "Have you passed it on?" "How could you have stopped it?"**

    "Suppose you are in your classroom and another student says that he heard your brother was in jail. What would you do? What would you say?"

3. ***Identify the Skill Components:*** (List on board or use sentence strips.)

    1. Ignore false rumors.
    2. Tell others to ignore false rumors.
    3. Never start false rumors.
    4. Keep false rumors from spreading.

4. ***Model the Skill:*** The teacher will model the skill by having a student tell the teacher a false rumor (e.g., We're going on a field trip today). Teacher models correct behavior in stopping a false rumor.

5. ***Behavioral Rehearsal:***

    A. *Selection:* Teacher selects two pairs of students to role play various situations.

    B. *Role Play:* Have children role play situations in which a false rumor is started, and appropriate behavior should be demonstrated. Role play should include situations that may occur in your classroom such as someone telling you that a classmate never takes a bath.

    C. *Completion:* After each role play, reinforce correct behavior, identify inappropriate behaviors, and reenact role play with corrections. When role play is done correctly, it is complete.

    D. *Reinforcers:* verbal encouragement, group reinforcement and non-verbal expressions of approval.

164

E. *Discussion:* Have children discuss role plays and any corrections that were made. Ask the class why it is important to prevent false rumors and stop them from spreading. Discuss the difficulties associated with these behaviors.

6. ***Practice:*** Give children copies of the following activity sheet, "The False Rumor." Have students make up a class-related false rumor in story form and have them explain how to stop a false rumor. Students will exchange papers and draw a picture of how they would react/feel if the false rumor were about them. Give copies of the accompanying activity sheet false rumor *bookmark patterns* to the children and have them color the bookmarks and cut out and paste them on cardboard.

7. ***Independent Use:***

A. Students will say, "That is just a false rumor; I will not spread it."

B. Students will relate to the teacher, "I stopped a false rumor."

8. ***Continuation:*** As related situations arise, teachers should point out that it is every person's responsibility to ignore false rumors and prevent them from spreading.

CHILDREN'S LITERATURE

Matthews, Judith. *Tuti, Blue Horse, and the Nipnope Man.* Morton Grove, IL: A. Whitman, 1993.

Mayer, Mercer. *There's a Nightmare in My Closet.* New York: Dial Books for Young Readers, 1985.

Name _____   Date _____

THE FALSE RUMOR

Directions: Make up a false rumor and write it down in complete sentences. Draw a picture to show how you would stop the false rumor.

A.   WRITE THE FALSE RUMOR HERE: _____

_____

_____

_____

_____

B.   DRAW YOUR PICTURE HERE TO SHOW HOW YOU WOULD STOP THE FALSE RUMOR.

BOOKMARK PATTERNS

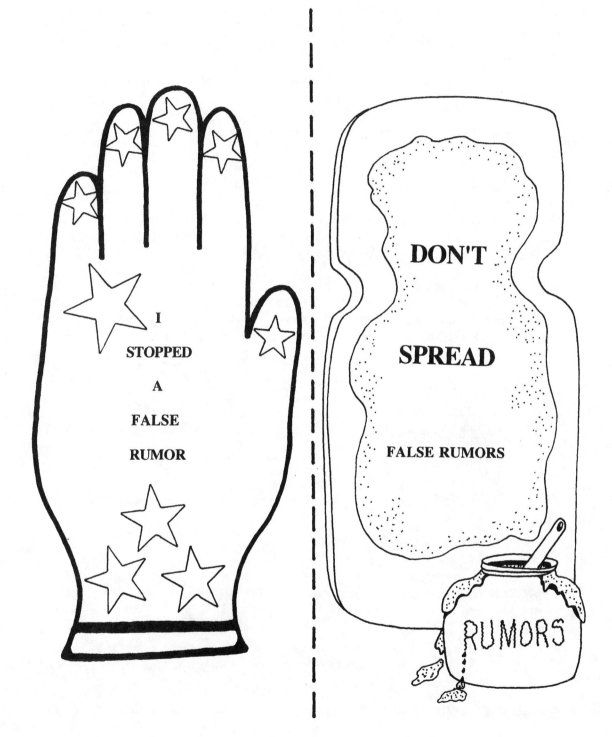

SOCIAL SKILL

Developing Strategies to Prevent False Rumors

Behavioral Objective: The children will recognize false rumors and develop strategies to prevent them.

Directed Lesson:

1. ***Establish the Need:*** Teacher initiates a discussion about ways to recognize rumors and the consequence of spreading them. Students should learn to identify with the feelings of others when the false rumors are aimed at destroying a person's character.

2. ***Introduction:*** Discuss the following questions with the class: **"Have you ever been accused of something you didn't do? How did you feel? Has someone ever said something about you to others that you wish hadn't been said? Why do people start rumors? Who starts rumors? How do people feel about someone who starts a rumor?"**

3. ***Identify the Skill Components:*** (List on board or on sentence strips.)

    1. Never start a false rumor.
    2. Avoid listening to rumors.
    3. Do not repeat and spread rumors.
    4. Try to erase the rumor.
    5. Say to the person wanting to tell you a rumor, "That's a rumor, and I will not listen to it."
    6. Tell others to ignore false rumors.
    7. Walk away.

4. ***Model the Skill:*** The teacher will demonstrate appropriate behavior when confronted with a rumor told by a student showing the skill steps listed.

5. ***Behavioral Rehearsal:***

    A. *Selection:* Teacher chooses two volunteer students to act out the following situations:

    B. *Role Play:*

    (1)*Student 1*—"Sally told me that Jane said Tammy was the most talkative girl on the school bus."

Student 2 —"I sit next to Tammy, and she rarely talks. Therefore, this must be a false rumor, and I am not going to listen to it." (Walks away.)

(2)*Student 1*—"Say, did you tell Bill about what happened to Steve?"

Student 2 —"No! I think it is a false rumor and I do not spread rumors. You shouldn't either, because someone could get hurt." (Walks away.)

C. *Completion:* After each role play, reinforce correct behavior. Identify inappropriate behaviors, and reenact role play with corrections. If there are no corrections, role play is complete.

D. *Reinforcers:* Verbal encouragement—"You did the right thing." "Good job!" Smile and nod head for approval. Have students in role play take a bow.

E. *Discussion:* Have the students discuss the role playing situations. "How did you feel when that happened?" Ask class why is it important to stop false rumors?

6. ***Practice:*** Give children copies of the activity sheet "Saying *NO* to Rumors" and read the directions to the class. Children can complete the activity sheets independently. Have a class discussion on them.

7. ***Independent Use:*** Distribute copies of the following home activity sheet, "Stopping Rumors." After children have drawn family members, and written the ways their family stops rumors, they should return the activity sheet to school for sharing with the class.

8. ***Continuation:*** Teacher reminds children of the hurt false rumors can cause, as related situations arise.

CHILDREN'S LITERATURE

Duvoisin, Roger. *Petunia.* New York: Knopf Books for Young Readers, 1962.

Scieszka, Jon. *The True Story of the Three Little Pigs.* New York: Viking Children's Books, 1989.

Name _____   Date _____

Saying NO to Rumors

Directions: Apply the skill steps and complete the cartoon below.

Name _____   Date _____

STOPPING RUMORS

Directions: Draw family members. What does your family say to rumors?

How Does Your Family Stop Rumors:

1. _____

2. _____

3. _____

4. _____

5. _____

SOCIAL SKILL

Learning to Ignore Distractions

Behavioral Objective: The children will remain on task by ignoring any distractions.

Directed Lesson:

1. **Establish the Need:** Teacher will initiate a discussion about the relevance and benefits of the skill. Stress that ignoring distractions allows for the completion of work in a shorter period of time.

2. **Introduction:** Read the following story:

   "Bobby was drying dishes for his mother. He was being ever so careful until all at once the telephone rang. Bobby jumped to run for the phone, and the dishes went crashing to the floor. If only Bobby had paid attention to what he was doing and not to the phone, mother's dishes would not now be in a hundred pieces."

   Ask Questions:

   "What did Bob do when the phone rang?"
   "What happened as a result?"
   "What attention do you give to a ringing phone?"
   "What could Bobby have done?"

3. **Identify the Skill Components:** (List on board before class.)

   1. Ignore distractions.
   2. Do not look at others.
   3. Do not listen to others.
   4. Stay on task.

4. **Model the Skill:** Teacher initiates discussion on the relevance and benefits of the skill. Stress that ignoring distractions allows for the completion of work in a shorter period of time and with no unforeseen accidents due to interruptions. Teacher can model the procedure for answering the telephone by first setting aside a task, and then answering the phone.

5. **Behavioral Rehearsal:**

   A. *Selection:* Teacher selects 2 groups of three children to role play.

   B. *Role Play:* Children will pair-up to play the following situations.

      1. Student is reading his library book and two friends are talking nearby.
      2. Student is standing in line and two others begin to push each other.

172

C. *Completion:* After each role play, reinforce correct behavior, identify inappropriate behaviors, and reenact role play with corrections. If there are no corrections, role play is complete.

D. *Reinforcers:* Give verbal praise to those children who follow skill components.

E. *Discussion:* Discuss difficulties in ignoring distractions.

6. *Practice:* Plan deliberate distractions (rustling papers, dropping pencil, etc.) and have children practice ignoring them. Award children who concentrate with a special badge like that on the following page.

7. *Independent Use:* Find out how someone at home has been distracted and what they have done to ignore the distraction. Be prepared to discuss this for the next lesson.

8. *Continuation:* Teachers should continually stress to children why it is important to concentrate—so that they can complete their work more quickly and go on to do other interesting things.

CHILDREN'S LITERATURE

Kessler, Leonard, *Here Comes the Strikeout.* New York: Harper Collins Children's Books, 1978.

I IGNORE DISTRACTIONS BADGE

Cut me out   **Wear me**

IGNORE DISTRACTIONS

SOCIAL SKILL
Remaining on Task

Behavioral Objective: The children will remain on task by ignoring any distractions.

Directed Lesson:

1. **Establish the Need:** Stress that ignoring distractions allows for the completion of a task in a shorter period of time.

2. **Introduction:** Read and discuss this poem.

    Don't let others disturb you . . .
    Don't let them get in the way . . .
    Your job is to get your work done
    And do just
    what the teachers say.

3. **Identify the Skill Components:** (List on board before class.)

    1. Ignore distractions.

    2. Do not look at others.

    3. Do not listen to others.

    4. Stay on task.

4. **Model the Skill:** Teacher relates what steps she/he should take to ignore distractions. (Turn away, close your eyes, don't make eye contact, think of something else, etc.)

5. **Behavioral Rehearsal:**

    A. *Selection:* Ask for volunteers. Time limits the number.

    B. *Role Play:* Have students read and role play ignored distractions brought from home. (If there are none that can be used, have students practice the skills that the teacher modeled in #4 above.)

    C. *Completion:* After each role play, reinforce correct behavior, identify inappropriate behaviors, and reenact role play with corrections. If there are no corrections, role play is complete.

    D. *Reinforcers:* Give verbal praise for shared situations where skill components were followed.

E. *Discussion:* Discuss how and why distractions were successfully ignored. Discuss successes in following skill components, such as being able to complete work, staying focused, not getting involved, staying out of mischief, etc.

6. *Practice:* Give children copies of the following activity sheet, "Scrambled Sentences," and have them unscramble the three mixed-up sentences.

7. *Independent Use:* Ask children to draw a picture that shows them successfully ignoring a distraction at home, (Eg., baby crying, siblings fighting, loud T.V., etc.). Then ask them to have a parent sign their drawing and bring their drawing to school.

8. *Continuation:* Teachers should remind children how much more quickly they can get work done if they develop the skill of ignoring distractions.

CHILDREN'S LITERATURE

Carle, Eric. *The Very Busy Spider.* New York: Putnam Publishing Group, 1989.

Name _____ Date _____

SCRAMBLED SENTENCES

Directions: Unscramble each of these mixed-up sentences. Write the unscrambled sentences on the blank lines.

1. look   others   at   not   DO

_____

2. listen others Do to not

_____

3. task on Stay

_____

SOCIAL SKILL
Concentrating on One's Work

Behavioral Objective: The children will remain on the task by ignoring any distractions.

Directed Lesson:

1. ***Establish the Need:*** The teacher initiates a discussion about the relevance and benefits of ignoring distractions. Stress that only by ignoring the distractions around us can we complete our work.

2. ***Introduction:*** Introduce the skill by reading the following story:

   "Myrtle the turtle was one of the best students in _____ school. She loved to read, write, add, and subtract. Even though she was a very good student, she was always nervous when she took a test. One morning her teacher surprised the class with a spelling quiz. Myrtle was very worried, even though she had studied all of the words. When the test began, Myrtle tried to concentrate on doing her best. Unfortunately, Jake the mouse was having a sneezing attack and it was disturbing Myrtle. She knew she had to ignore the sneezing by not looking or listening to Jake. It worked! Myrtle got all her spelling words right."

3. ***Identify the Skill Components:*** (List on board before class.)

   1. Concentrate on your work.
   2. Ignore distractions.
   3. Do not look at others while you are working.
   4. Do not listen to others while you are working.
   5. Continue working.

4. ***Model the Skill:*** Teacher models the skill steps by having a child try to distract her while she works on a paper. Stress to the class that you can ignore someone and concentrate on what you are working on.

5. ***Behavioral Rehearsal:***

   A. *Selection:* Select five pairs of students to role play.

   B. *Role Play:* Each pair of students will role play acceptable activities that can distract others. One child will be doing an assignment, one the activity that is distracting. The first child will ignore the other by not turning around and looking or listening to him/her. Then reverse roles.

C. *Completion:* After each role play, reinforce correct behavior, identify inappropriate behaviors, and reenact role play with corrections. If there are no corrections, role play is complete.

D. *Reinforcers:* verbal encouragement, tangible rewards, physical display of approval (i.e., hug, pat, smile), teacher will read a story to the group.

E. *Discussion:* Have the class discuss the role plays and the corrections that were made. Discuss the importance of ignoring distractions and the difficulties that the children have with the skill.

6. **Practice:** Distribute copies of the following activity sheet, "Ignoring Distractions," to complete. They must pretend to want to read a library book in the lunchroom after eating. They must write down the distractions they might have and what they did about them.

7. **Independent Use:**

A. Have the class write down what types of distractions they have at home while doing their homework. Also, how they were able to ignore them and complete their work.

B. Children can keep a record of distractions in the classroom for a week and what they did about them.

8. **Continuation:** Teachers should continue to encourage children to ignore distractions and concentrate on the task at hand.

CHILDREN'S LITERATURE

Bunting, Eve. *The Valentine Bears.* Boston: Houghton Mifflin, 1985.

Name_____   Date _____

IGNORING DISTRACTIONS

Directions: Suppose that you want to take a library book to the lunchroom to read when you finish eating. What kind of distractions might you have? How could you ignore them?

#1 DISTRACTION: _____

" WELL, I COULD _____

_____

_____ "

#2 DISTRACTION: _____

" HMMM, I COULD _____

_____ "

#3 DISTRACTION: _____

" THIS IS MY PLAN _____

_____

_____ "

Let's Read!

SOCIAL SKILL

Ignoring Distractions in the Classroom

Behavioral Objective: The children will ignore distractions in the classroom and continue working.

Directed Lesson:

1. **Establish the Need:** Teacher initiates a discussion about how ignoring distractions permits us to complete necessary work.

2. **Introduction:** Teacher will ask the following questions, and list answers on the board. **"What interrupts you when you are doing class work?" "If we can't stop the interruption what can we do?" "Why is it important that we learn to concentrate and ignore distractions?"**

3. **Identify the Skill Components:** (List on board before class.)

    1. Ignore distractions.
    2. Do not listen.
    3. Look away.
    4. Continue working.

4. **Model the Skill:** Teacher will model a student working at his/her desk. Two students will role play talking at the door about a safety assembly. Teacher will ignore the distraction and continue working.

5. **Behavioral Rehearsal:**

    A. *Selection:* Teacher will select five students to model student working and another five to model distractions listed on the board (from the introduction).

    B. *Role Play:* Teacher will identify one student at a time who is to be working in front of the room. Then have the other students role play distractions.

    C. *Completion:* After each role play, reinforce correct behavior, identify inappropriate behaviors, and reenact role play with corrections. If there are no corrections, role play is complete.

    D. *Reinforcers:* verbal encouragement, tangible rewards, smile and nod head to show approval.

    E. *Discussion:* Have students discuss the role plays and the corrections that were made. Ask why it is important to ignore distractions.

6. ***Practice:*** Distribute copies of the following reproducible, "Distraction Monster Badge," to each student and have them color it.

7. ***Independent Use:*** Students will write about how they ignored distractions, pets, phone, sisters, brothers, etc., when doing homework.

8. ***Continuation:*** Teachers should continue to remind students of the benefits that come from being able to ignore distractions while doing one's work.

CHILDREN'S LITERATURE

Allard, Harry. *Miss Nelson Is Missing.* Boston: Houghton Mifflin, 1993.

DISTRACTION MONSTER BADGE

I try to get your attention

Distraction Monster

JUST IGNORE ME!

Cut it out

color it

SOCIAL SKILL
Ignoring Distractions (Review)

Behavioral Objective: The children will ignore distractions and continue working.

Directed Lesson:

1. ***Establish the Need:*** Teacher reviews importance of ignoring distractions from the previous lesson.

2. ***Introduction:*** Teacher tells the story of how students had a contest to complete a creative art project within a two-hour limit. The students who won the contest were the ones who could ignore the noise from the construction outside. The winner won a trip to the Art Museum.

3. ***Identify the Skill Components:*** (List on board before class.)

    1. Ignore distractions.
    2. Do not listen.
    3. Look away.
    4. Continue working.

4. ***Model the Skill:*** Teacher models skill steps by continuing board work (math examples) while ignoring classroom distractions. (Distractions: T.V., music, children laughing).

5. ***Behavioral Rehearsal:***

    A. *Selection:* Teacher will select four students to role play.

    B. *Role Play:* Two students will continue to work while two neighbors talk about last night's T.V. movie.

    C. *Completion:* After each role play, reinforce correct behavior, identify inappropriate behaviors, and reenact role play with corrections. If there are no corrections, role play is complete.

    D. *Reinforcers:* verbal encouragement, smile and nod head to show approval.

    E. *Discussion:* Have students discuss the role plays and the corrections that were made. Ask class why it is important to ignore distractions.

6. ***Practice:*** Give students copies of the following activity sheet, "Balloon Bubble Talk," to complete by filling in the balloons.

184

7. ***Independent Use:*** Have parents sign a note stating that their child ignored distractions from the phone, T.V., etc. while doing his/her homework.

8. ***Continuation:*** Teachers should continue to point out the value of being able to attend to task as situations arise.

CHILDREN'S LITERATURE

DePaola, Tomie. *Tomie DePaola's Book of Poems.* New York: Putnam Publishing Group.

Silverstein, Shel. *Where the Sidewalk Ends.* New York: Dell, 1986.

Name _____   Date _____

BALLOON BUBBLE TALK

Directions: What can you say to a classmate who is disturbing you when you are trying to work? Fill in the bubbles.

SOCIAL SKILL
Giving a Deserved Compliment

Behavioral Objective: The child will give a deserved compliment to someone he/she selects.

Directed Lesson:

1. **Establish the Need:** Teacher will initiate a discussion about the relevance and benefits of the skill. Stress that giving a compliment to a person helps improve their self-image. It also makes the person who gives the compliment feel good about himself/herself because he/she did something nice.

2. **Introduction:** Read this poem to the class:

> **Have you ever met someone**
> **Special and extra nice,**
> **Who is always there to help you**
> **Maybe once and maybe twice?**
> **Look around very carefully**
> **To find the deserving one**
> **Give them the compliment that's true**
> **And they will be a friend to you!**

3. **Identify the Skill Components:** (List on board before class.)

   1. Select someone to compliment.
   2. Decide what nice thing you will say.
   3. Make sure the compliment is true.
   4. Think of how you will say it.
   5. Say the compliment.

4. **Model the Skill:** (Teacher models correct behavior.) Teacher gives student a deserved compliment. (Eg: "Your handwritten paper looks very neat.")

5. **Behavioral Rehearsal:**

   A. *Selection:* Teacher selects four pairs of children to role play.

   B. *Role Play:* Children will role play giving compliments in these areas. Physical appearance, school work, something nice they did for somebody, and something nice they said to someone.

    C. *Completion:* After each role play, reinforce correct behavior, identify inappropriate behaviors, and reenact role play with corrections. If there are no corrections, role play is complete.

    D. *Reinforcers:* Give verbal praise to those children who follow the skill components. Discuss why you compliment them for giving good compliments. Also give them a "Good Compliment" Badge.

    E. *Discussion:* Discuss problems with giving a compliment, for example that you feel shy or the receiver does not accept it graciously. But, encourage giving a compliment daily.

6. **Practice:** Give children copies of the following activity sheet, "My Compliment." They are to think of someone to compliment, draw a picture of him/her, and write the compliment underneath.

7. **Independent Use:** Ask children to give a compliment to three people outside of school, then be prepared to repeat their compliments in class.

8. **Continuation:** Teachers should remind children that compliments make both persons feel good—the person who gives the compliment and the person who receives it!

CHILDREN'S LITERATURE

Aliki. *Communication.* New York: Greenwillow, 1993.

Name _____   Date _____

MY COMPLIMENT

Directions: Read the poem. Draw a picture in the mirror of the person to whom you wish to give a compliment. Then give it!

Mirror, mirror on the wall
Give a compliment and that's not all,
Make it nice and make it kind
A deserving person is not hard to find.

SOCIAL SKILL
Giving a Compliment

Behavioral Objective: Each child will give a deserved compliment to someone he/she selects.

Directed Lesson:

1. **Establish the Need:** Teacher initiates discussion on the merits of giving deserved compliments to others. It helps build confidence in other people and makes the person giving the compliment feel good too. It also helps establish better relationships with others. The more positive a person is towards others, the better others feel about that person.

2. **Introduction:** Read this poem to the class:

    > **You look nice and that is true.**
    > **I like your shirt of baby blue.**
    > **Your hair is brushed and looks so shiny.**
    > **Your teeth are white and oh so tiny.**
    > **"May I please?" are words you say.**
    > **And you use them every day.**
    > **There's one more thing that I must tell**
    > **It's that you read your stories well.**
    > **All the things I've said to you**
    > **Are absolutely true, true, true!**

    Ask the children what they think the poem means. Stress that all of the compliments were true. None of them were made up. Also, people know when you are not giving them a compliment they deserve. Most people want to be appreciated for who they are, not someone they are not.

3. **Identify the Skill Components:** (List on board before class.)

    1. Select someone to compliment.
    2. Decide what nice thing you will say.
    3. Make sure the compliment is true.
    4. How will you say it?
    5. Say the compliment.

4. **Model the Skill:** The teacher will model the skill by selecting a child to give a deserved compliment to. It would be best to pick someone who has an obvious good point, for example, some child who has a good paper on display in the classroom.

5. ***Behavioral Rehearsal:***

    A. *Selection:* Teacher selects ten children to role play.

    B. *Role Play:* Children will each select a child to compliment. They must point out the child and give the reason why the child was selected. Then, say the compliment.

    C. *Completion:* After each role play, reinforce correct behavior, identify inappropriate behaviors, and reenact role play with corrections. If there are no corrections, role play is complete.

    D. *Reinforcers:* If the child gives an appropriate compliment, the teacher should congratulate him on his skill. The other children will hopefully reinforce with praise. A sticker or certificate is a positive reinforcer.

    E. *Discussion:* Have the class discuss the importance of giving a deserved compliment to others. Ask how each role player felt giving and receiving compliments.

6. ***Practice:*** Give children copies of the following activity sheet, "Three Magic Compliments," to complete.

7. ***Independent Use:*** It's "Compliment Time." Every morning in school, one child should volunteer to compliment another child on something that occurred in the classroom.

8. ***Continuation:*** Teachers will encourage children to give deserved compliments to others as a daily practice.

CHILDREN'S LITERATURE

Lewis, J. Patrick. *July Is a Mad Mosquito.* New York: Macmillan Children's Group, 1994.

Silverstein, Shel. *A Light in the Attic.* New York: Harper Collins Children's Books, 1981.

A TEACHER'S GUIDESHEET
TO BEING POSITIVE

"PAY ATTENTION TO THE POSITIVE"

WAYS TO SAY "GOOD!"

Good thinking!
Nice going!
That's the way!
Great Job!
You're the best!
You're an angel!
You are right!
Keep it up!
You're learning fast!
Good for you!
You're doing beautifully!
Great try!
Way to go!
You remembered!
Outstanding!
Much better!
Thanks for helping
SUPER!
You've got it down pat!
Congratulations!
What a great idea!
LOOKING GOOD!
I'm impressed!
You're doing fine!
Superb work!
Thanks a million!
I'm proud of you!
You did it!!!
Better than ever!
What a champ!

How clever!
Terrific!
Wonderful!
Hurrah for you!
Exceptional!
Better than ever!
Look at you go!
Sensational!
Thanks for sharing!
What careful work!
I knew you could do it!
How original!
You're a real friend!
Exactly right!
You're on the right track!
Perfect!
How thoughtful!
Keep up the good work!
How nice of you!
You're a gem!
You're one in a million!
You've made progress!
I love it!
You're improving every day!
You're on the right track!
You'll make your mother proud!
Good Boy!   Good Girl!
That was nice of you!
Thank you very much!

AND you can think of a MILLION MORE!

Name _____   Date _____

THREE MAGIC COMPLIMENTS

Directions: Select 3 people in your classroom that you want to give a compliment to. Write their name, and the compliment. Share these in class.

NAME   COMPLIMENT

1._____   _____

2._____   _____

3._____   _____

Giving a compliment
is like giving a
present!

SOCIAL SKILL
Giving a Verbal Compliment

Behavioral Objective: Children will verbally compliment another person.

Directed Lesson:

1. **Establish the Need:** Teacher initiates a discussion about how giving a compliment makes you and the receiver feel good.

2. **Introduction:** Ask students how they feel when someone gives them a compliment. List on board: **"What things have you been complimented for?"** Ask, **"How do you feel when you receive a compliment?"** Ask and list responses on the board. **"What behaviors deserve a compliment?"**

3. **Identify the Skill Components:** (List on board before class.)

    1. Decide what and who to compliment.

    2. Determine how to phrase it.

    3. Give the compliment.

4. **Model the Skill:** Teacher will model giving compliments for schoolwork, appearance, behavior, etc. to four students in the classroom.

5. **Behavioral Rehearsal:**

    A. *Selection:* Teacher will select ten students to role play.

    B. *Role Play:* Each child will compliment his/her neighbor.

    C. *Completion:* After each role play, reinforce correct behavior, identify inappropriate behaviors, and reenact role play with corrections. If there are no corrections, role play is complete.

    D. *Reinforcers:* verbal praise, physical smile and nod head to show approval.

    E. *Discussion:* Have children discuss the role plays and corrections that were made. Ask class why compliments are necessary and important.

6. **Practice:** Distribute copies of the following "Compliment Certificate" for students to complete.

7. **Independent Use:** Teacher will ask class to share during recess, compliments they will give to family members.

8.   ***Continuation:*** Remind children that giving a compliment makes both the giver and the receiver feel good.

CHILDREN'S LITERATURE

Cummings, Pat. *Clean Your Room, Harvey Moon!* New York: Macmillan Children's Group, 1994.

COMPLIMENT CERTIFICATE

COMPLIMENTS TO:

FOR:

SOCIAL SKILL

Asking Permission to Borrow Property

Behavioral Objective: The children will get the owner's consent before borrowing property and belongings and will return it without damage.

Directed Lesson:

1. **Establish the Need:** Teacher stresses that no one likes having his/her property and belongings taken without giving permission. Also, emphasize that not taking care of property can lead to problems.

2. **Introduction:** Read this poem to the class:

    > **If you don't have something . . .**
    > **something you really need,**
    > **You must ask permission to borrow**
    > **and then if you succeed**
    > **be extra extra careful**
    > **with that which is on loan**
    > **until you're sure you've got it safely back at home.**

    Teacher asks class about the meaning of the poem.

3. **Identify the Skill Components:** (List on board before class.)

    1. Ask for permission to borrow something.
    2. Wait for "yes" answer.
    3. Don't take it if answer is "no."
    4. Take good care of borrowed items.
    5. When finished, return them in good condition.

4. **Model the Skill:** (Teacher models correct behavior.) Refer to skill steps on board. Teacher should model asking for and receiving requested property. "May I borrow your glue to build my tepee for our social studies project?" "Thank you for the glue." (Pretend to use it, and return it.)

5. **Behavioral Rehearsal:**

    A. *Selection:* Teacher selects five pairs of children to role play.

    B. *Role Play:* Children will role play asking to borrow pencils, crayons, rulers, erasers, and paper.

   C. *Completion:* After each role play, reinforce correct behavior, identify inappropriate behaviors, and reenact role play with corrections. If there are no corrections, role play is complete.

   D. *Reinforcers:* Give verbal praise to those children who follow the skill components. Also give "Good Borrower Certificates." Teachers and students compliment children doing role play correctly.

> **"Juan, I liked the way you asked to borrow Nancy's ruler."**
> **"Scott, I liked the way you let Andre borrow _____."**

   E. *Discussion:* Discuss the importance of asking permission and the consequences of not asking for permission. Also emphasize the need to take care of borrowed property.

6. **Practice:** Have children complete copies of the following activity sheet, "Borrowing a Bike," and check their work.

7. **Independent Use:** Setup a materials shelf with items that may be borrowed (pencils, eraser, scissors). Write down name, what was borrowed, and in what condition it was returned. Have note signed by borrower. Stress that students may use this skill whenever borrowing and lending in any setting.

8. **Continuation:** Teachers should point out the importance of being a good borrower as related situations arise.

CHILDREN'S LITERATURE

Oxenbury, Helen. *Mother's Helper.* New York: Dial Books for Young Readers, 1991.

Van Allsburg, Chris. *Two Bad Ants.* Boston: Houghton Mifflin, 1988.

Name _____   Date _____

BORROWING A BIKE

Directions: You would like to borrow your friend's bike. In the first bike wheel, copy what you should say to your friend. In the second bike wheel, copy words that describe the bike when it is returned.

1. HOW TO ASK:

A. I'm taking your bike.
B. May I borrow your bike?
C. Give me your bike!

2. HOW SHOULD THE BIKE LOOK WHEN IT IS RETURNED?

A. flat tire
B. bent frame
C. good shape

SOCIAL SKILL

Asking Permission Before Borrowing

Behavioral Objective: The children will get the owner's permission *before* borrowing property and then return it without damage.

Directed Lesson:

1. **Establish the Need:** Teacher initiates a discussion of the relevance and benefits of the skill. Stress that unless you get permission from the owner to borrow the property, it is stealing. Stealing is wrong. How would you like it if your property was stolen? What might happen if people just took what they wanted from others?

2. **Introduction:** Read the following story to the class:

    "One day in Mr. Frank's classroom the children heard a very strange sound. It was like the humming of a machine. Suddenly, a little spaceship appeared at the window outside of their classroom. Mr. Frank opened the window and invited the stranger in. After it landed on the floor, the door opened and a space creature emerged. He looked like a frog. He told the class that he was from another planet and wanted to go to school on Earth. The class welcomed him and he sat next to Ruth. Mr. Frank gave the children a math assignment to do. The frog creature had no materials so he just went into Ruth's desk and took paper and pencils. Because he didn't know how to use the pencils, he kept breaking them. Pretty soon there were no pencils to use. Ruth was very upset and explained to him that on Earth, everyone asked permission to borrow other people's property. She would gladly have loaned him a pencil and explained how to use it so that he would not have broken so many. The frog creature said he understood. The next assignment was a picture to color. He turned to Ruth and asked to borrow her crayons. She not only lent them, but showed him how to use them without breaking them. When he was finished, he returned the crayons in perfect shape. When the frog creature was ready to leave, he told everyone that he would teach his friends on his planet to ask permission before borrowing. He thought it was a great idea!"

3. **Identify the Skill Components:** (List on board before class.)

    1. Ask if you can borrow an item.
    2. Wait for an answer of *yes.*
    3. If the answer is *no,* do not take it.
    4. Be careful with it.
    5. Return it in good condition when finished.

4. ***Model the Skill:*** The teacher will model the skill by asking one of the students if he/she can borrow a pencil. The teacher will then return it undamaged as soon as he/she is finished with it.

5. ***Behavioral Rehearsal:***

   A. *Selection:* Teacher selects four pairs of children to role play.

   B. *Role Play:* Students role play a situation in which one child wants to borrow something from the other child. They must follow the skill steps for correctly borrowing another person's property.

   C. *Completion:* After each role play, reinforce correct behavior, identify inappropriate behaviors, and reenact role play with corrections. If there are no corrections, role play is complete.

   D. *Reinforcers:* After each role play, the teacher should encourage correct behaviors with praise. Start a "Good Neighbor Club" in the classroom and have children list ways that they can help one another. Have a membership card for each child.

   E. *Discussion:* Discuss the possible consequences of not asking for permission before taking another person's property. How would they feel if it happened to them? Discuss the role plays and problems connected with this skill.

6. ***Practice:*** Distribute copies of the following activity sheet, "Freddie and Titus." Children will match the skill steps for the fish and turtle to follow. They will write down which expression each one would use. Freddie is the one asking permission to borrow an item.

   Freddie the fish: 1. May I borrow your book?

   5. Here it is, I returned it in good condition.

   Titus the Turtle: 2. Yes, you may borrow my book.

   3. No, you may not borrow my book right now.

   4. Please be careful with the book.

7. ***Independent Use:*** Children will ask permission every morning before borrowing property. The teacher will reinforce and praise continually.

8. ***Continuation:*** Teachers will continue to point out to children that borrowing someone else's property without their permission is stealing, and wrong.

CHILDREN'S LITERATURE

Corey, Dorothy. *Everybody Takes Turns.* Morton Grove, IL: A. Whitman.

Name _____ Date _____

FREDDIE AND TITUS

Directions: Rewrite the 5 sentences below in the proper spaces. Would Freddie be saying this? Would Titus be saying this? Think carefully about their conversation.

1. May I borrow your book?

2. Yes, you may borrow my book.

3. No, you may not borrow my book right now.

4. Please be careful with the book.

5. Here it is, I returned it in good condition.

FREDDIE THE FISH SAYS:

_____

_____

_____

_____

TITUS THE TURTLE SAYS:

_____

_____

_____

_____

_____

SOCIAL SKILL
Respecting Other's Property

Behavioral Objective: Children will ask permission to borrow a classmate's supplies.

Directed Lesson:

1. **Establish the Need:** Teacher initiates a discussion about how the very act of asking permission shows we respect other people's property.

2. **Introduction:** Ask students: **"How do you feel when someone takes something of yours without asking first?" "What is the proper way of asking to borrow something?"**

3. **Identify the Skill Components:** (List on board before class.)

    1. Think of what you need to borrow.
    2. Say "May I please borrow . . .?"
    3. Wait for an answer.
    4. Return after use in good condition.

4. **Model the Skill:** Teacher uses the puppets to model the skill, asking and answering questions appropriately. "May I please borrow your _____?" "Yes you may" or "no you may not because . . .").

5. **Behavioral Rehearsal:**

    A. *Selection:* The teacher will select ten students who will ask permission to borrow something from a classmate.

    B. *Role Play:* Students will role play, following the listed skill components. Student will ask to borrow items.

    C. *Completion:* After each role play, reinforce correct behavior, identify inappropriate behaviors, and reenact role play with corrections. If there are no corrections, role play is complete.

    D. *Reinforcers:* verbal encouragement and tangible rewards; approval indicated by nod of head and smile.

    E. *Discussion:* Have children discuss the role plays and the corrections that were made. Be sure that the class sees the need for asking permission when borrowing items.

6. **Practice:** Use the accompanying activity sheet, "May I Please?"

7. ***Independent Use:*** Teacher will encourage students to ask permission to borrow something at home. Report to class what was borrowed and how permission was asked and in what condition it was returned.

8. ***Continuation:*** Remind students that they should always obtain permission to use another's property as related situations arise.

CHILDREN'S LITERATURE

Dexter, Catherine. *Gertie's Green Thumb.* New York: Dell, 1988.

Name _____   Date _____

MAY I PLEASE?

Directions: Complete each sentence. Then read a sentence to a classmate, and play the MAY I BORROW game.   First student asks a question. Second student answers, "Yes you may." First student says, "Thank you."

1. Mother, may I borrow _____

_____?

2. Father, may I please borrow _____

_____?

3. Mrs. _____, may I borrow _____

_____?

4. _____, may I borrow _____

_____?

5. _____, may I borrow _____

_____?

SOCIAL SKILL

Understanding Each Person's Uniqueness

Behavioral Objective: The student will learn to accept that each person is unique. The student will further learn to understand that we are alike in many ways. However, we must accept each other for our individual differences.

Directed Lesson:

1. **Establish the Need:** Discuss the relevance and benefits of the skill. Children need to know that we are all different and that it's *OK* to be different. (However, in many ways we are all alike.) When we acknowledge these differences as being OK, we interact with each other in a more positive way and we continue to have a positive self-image.

2. **Introduction:** Teacher asks:

    > **"Are we all the same height?**
    > **Do we all like the same foods?**
    > **Do we all live in the same house?**
    > **Do we all have the same favorite T.V. program?**
    > **Do we all have the same favorite color?**
    > **Do we all have the same favorite toy?"**

    Have comparisons made of pencils, apples, oranges, etc., by having the children examine their own items *very* closely, looking for 1 or 2 unique features. Then put all items from each category together in one area and see if the children can find their own pencil, apple, orange, etc.

3. **Identify the Skill Components:** (List on board before class or on sentence strips.)

    1. List some likenesses.
    2. List some differences.
    3. Define unique.
    4. Define what is unique about *you?*
    5. Realize that it is OK to be different and unique.
    6. Decide how you should react to these differences.

4. *Model the Skill:* Read the following poem to children:

Different and Alike

I'm me
I'm like everyone
I'm different from everyone
I'm even UNIQUE

You're you
You're like everyone

You're different from everyone
You're UNIQUE

Alike as we are
Different as we are
We should all be treated the same
We should treat all others the same

5. *Behavioral Rehearsal:*

   A. *Selection:* Teach entire class the poem.

   B. *Role Play:* Select children to come up and recite the poem in groups of five.

   C. *Completion:* Point out differences in groups after recitation.

   D. *Reinforcers:* Present "I Am Unique" badges (see the following page). Have children decorate their badge. (Make it unique.)

   E. *Discussion:* Have class recall the positive unique feature of each student as badges are pinned on each individual.

6. *Practice:* Teacher has sample activity sheet, "Plant Your Flower Garden," with flowers of same size and colored identically. Teacher asks, **"Aren't the flowers pretty? How can we make them even prettier or more unique?"** Distribute the activity sheet and encourage children to create flowers of different size and to color the flowers differently.

7. *Independent Use:*

   A. Give children copies of the following home activity sheet, "What makes family members unique?" Have them fill in what makes members of their family (even pets) unique.

   B. Return papers and discuss findings.

8. *Continuation:* Teacher reminds students of continued positive relationships when this skill is used. Review poem.

CHILDREN'S LITERATURE

Neitzel, Dorothy. *The Dress I'll Wear to the Party.* New York: Greenwillow, 1992.

I AM UNIQUE BADGE

Directions: Color your badge with your favorite colors. Think of the very polite response you will give when people ask, "Why are you wearing that badge?"

Draw your picture in the center.

PLANT YOUR FLOWER GARDEN

Directions: Make all of the flowers a different size, shape and color. One thinks it is more beautiful than the others. What lesson does the flower have to learn?

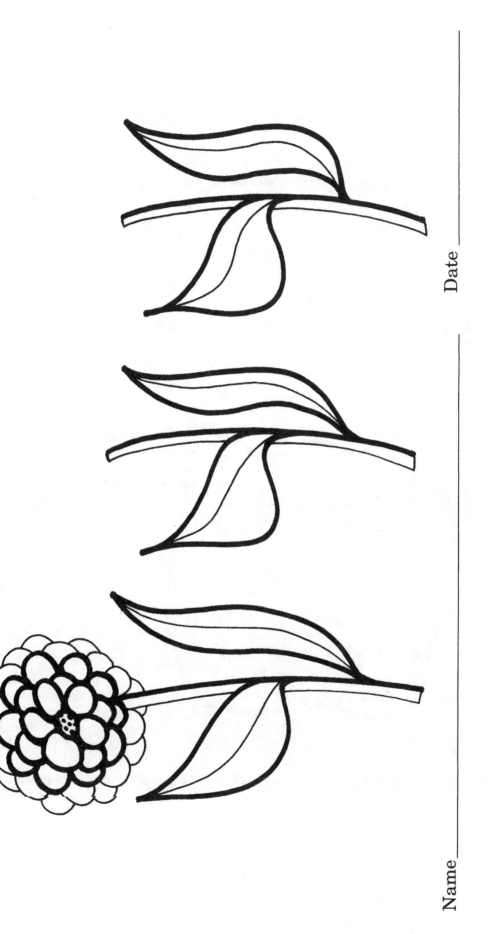

Name _____

Date _____

Name _____   Date _____

WHAT MAKES FAMILY MEMBERS UNIQUE?

Directions: Draw pictures of four different members of your family in the spaces below. Include pets. Show how each person or pet is unique.

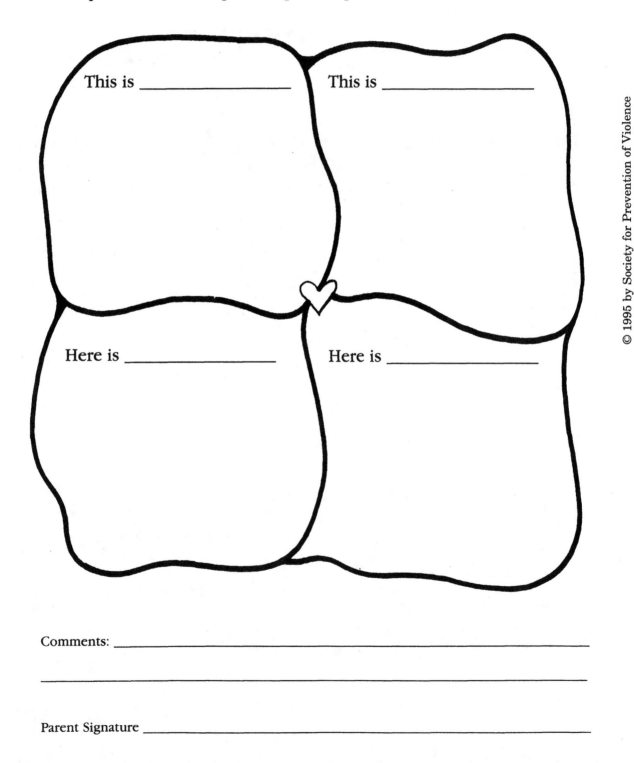

This is _____

This is _____

Here is _____

Here is _____

Comments: _____

_____

Parent Signature _____

ACCEPTING DIFFERENCES

SOCIAL SKILL
Recognizing Individual Differences

Behavioral Objective: The children will be able to recognize, accept and appreciate individual differences.

Directed Lesson:

1. **Establish the Need:** The teacher initiates a discussion about the relevance and benefits of the skill. It is important to display a tolerance for an individual with characteristics different from one's own, by accepting the person without derogatory comments or actions.

2. **Introduction:** The teacher relates the story of an ugly caterpillar:

   "Once upon a time there was an ugly caterpillar. All the birds and other animals made fun of him, because he was so ugly." Discuss how the others treated him and how the caterpillar felt. **"One day the caterpillar made a cocoon for himself because he was so unhappy. A few months later, out came a beautiful butterfly."** Discuss feelings of other birds, caterpillars and butterflies.

3. **Identify the Skill Components:** (List on board or use sentence strips.)

   1. Realize that everyone is different to some degree.

   2. Keep from saying unkind words or acting badly towards others.

   3. Be kind to others, especially those who are different from you.

   4. Each of us needs to be liked and treated well.

4. **Model the Skill:** The teacher models the skill by using two animal puppets in two different situations, illustrating the skill components.

5. **Behavioral Rehearsal:**

   A. *Selection:* Teacher selects six students; five are four-legged animals and one is a snake.

   B. *Role Play:* Have students role play this situation: five animals want to play basketball but the teams are uneven. The snake approaches but no one wants him on their team because he has no arms or legs to bounce the ball. Teacher should motivate the group to let the snake play since the snake has unique abilities (e.g., snake can block ball by standing on his tail).

   C. *Completion:* After role play, reinforce correct behavior, identify prejudicial attitudes, and reenact role play with corrections. If there are no corrections, role play is complete.

D. *Reinforcers:* verbal praise, group reinforcement, non-verbal expressions of approval.

E. *Discussion:* Have the class discuss the importance of treating children who are different from them with kindness. Without behaving in a negative way or making an issue of the difference, emphasize that everyone is unique.

6. ***Practice:*** Have children complete the following story sheet, "A New Fish on the Block," by composing a story about the fish who is different. Students can work together.

7. ***Independent Use:*** Distribute the independent activity sheet, "Something Unique," for students to complete at home. They are to write down what they think is unique about a family member, a friend and a peer, then return the worksheet for discussion in class.

8. ***Continuation:*** Teacher should continue to remind students that each of us is different in one way or another. We should all be tolerant of each other's differences.

CHILDREN'S LITERATURE

Rubel, Nicole. *Cyrano the Bear.* New York: Dial Books for Young Readers, 1995.

Varley, Susan. *Badger's Parting Gifts.* New York: Wm. Morrow, 1992.

Name _____   Date _____

A NEW FISH ON THE BLOCK

Compose a story about the different fish who came to school one day. Write it in the water below.

Name _____   Date _____

SOMETHING UNIQUE

Directions: Write three complete sentences telling something unique about a family member, a friend, and a peer.

_____

_____

_____

_____

_____

_____

_____

_____

_____

SOCIAL SKILL
Preventing Prejudice

Behavioral Objective: The children will recognize, accept and appreciate individual differences.

Directed Lesson:

1. **Establish the Need:** Teacher discusses individual differences with the class **"There are no two people alike. Everyone is different in some way. We must learn to accept people for who they are, and appreciate them as people regardless of their differences."**

2. **Introduction:** Teacher asks the following: **"Do all of us wear our hair the same way? Are we all the same size and height?"** Teacher reads the following story:

    "A new student from the South comes to the third grade class at our school. The teacher introduces the student to the class, and asks him to tell something about himself. When the new student begins to talk, the class starts laughing."

    Teacher asks, **"Why did the class react the way they did? How do you think the new student felt?"** Teacher could then initiate a discussion about regional differences in speech patterns.

3. **Identify the Skill Components:** (List skills on board or use sentence strips.)

    1. Think and realize that all people are different.
    2. Learn to know people by talking to them.
    3. Play with them.
    4. Let them eat at your table.
    5. Invite them to be part of the group.

4. **Model the Skill:** Teacher chooses one student to pretend to be a newcomer to the U.S.A., coming from Japan. The teacher then models the skill steps listed.

5. **Behavioral Rehearsal:**

    A. *Selection:* Teacher places the following role play parts on index cards for students to read. Teacher then selects two puppets and two students to interact the following situation.

    B. *Role Play:* 1st Student - "David, I hear that you're from Japan. Come and sit next to me at lunchtime, and let's talk about your country. When we go out to play, I'll introduce you to our baseball team. OK?"

2nd Student—"Thank you Tommy. You really make me feel a part of the class, even though I am from a different country."

   C. *Completion:* Discuss role play, reinforcing appropriate behavior and correcting inappropriate responses. If there are no corrections, role play is complete.

   D. *Reinforcers:* Verbal encouragement - **"I really like the way you made him/her feel a part of the group." "It really makes me feel good to see you react that way." Smile and nod for approval.**

   E. *Discussion:* Students will react to role play, and suggest improvements and benefits.

6.   **Practice:** Give students copies of the following activity sheet, "Alike and Different." Read through the directions, have students complete the activity, and share responses.

7.   **Independent Use:** Pass out tagboard puppet models of the four animal puppets on the following two pages. Have students cut out and color the patterns and paste them on popsicle sticks. Then have students write on their animals how they are *unique* (different from each other). Have the children come up in pairs and share with each other how they are different.

8.   **Continuation:** Teacher tells students, **"You can make people feel accepted by letting them become a part of your group. This makes persons feel included, and makes them feel good about themselves."** Teacher should continue pointing out the need for this skill as related situations arise.

CHILDREN'S LITERATURE

Belton, Sandra. *May'naise Sandwiches and Sunshine Tea.* New York: Macmillan (Four Winds), 1994.

Linden, Anne Marie. *Emerald Blue.* New York: Macmillan (Atheneum), 1994.

Name _____   Date _____

ALIKE AND DIFFERENT

Directions: List ways in which people are _alike._
List ways in which people are _different_.

ALIKE:

1. _____

2. _____

3. _____

4. _____

5. _____

DIFFERENT:

1. _____

2. _____

3. _____

4. _____

5. _____

ANIMAL PUPPETS - I

Color and cut out the dog and the duck. Tape them to flat sticks. Use these puppets to tell how each one is unique.

ANIMAL PUPPETS - II

Color and cut out the pig and the horse. Tape them to flat sticks. Use them as puppets and have them talk about how each one is unique.

SOCIAL SKILL
Learning to Say "NO!"

Behavioral Objective: The children will say no when pressured by peers to do something they don't want to do.

Directed Lesson:

1. **Establish the Need:** The teacher initiates a discussion pertaining to making one's own choices and feeling free to say no if that is the choice.

2. **Introduction:** Teacher can read the following:

   "**Everyone from _____ school was going to watch the _____ (big game, dance contest, talent show, etc.: choose one). They called for Beth to hurry. Beth knew Mom wanted her to watch little sister Mandy. She could always go and say she forgot. What should she do?**

3. **Identify the Skill Components:** (List on board before class.)

   1. Think about what other children want you to do.
   2. Decide why you don't want or cannot do it.
   3. Say no in a nice way.
   4. If asked, tell why you won't or cannot do.

4. **Model the Skill:** (Teacher models correct behavior.) *Eg:* All the children from school are going _____. They are laughing and having a good time and call to say they are leaving now. I have my work to finish. I really want to go. Since my work is not done, I will say "I cannot go this time."

5. **Behavioral Rehearsal:**

   A. *Selection:* Teacher selects a group of children and an individual child.

   B. *Role Play:* The group will try to persuade the individual child to do something that he or she does not necessarily want to do or cannot do at that time.

   C. *Completion:* After each role play, reinforce correct behavior, identify inappropriate behaviors, and reenact role play with corrections. If there are no corrections, role play is complete.

   D. *Reinforcers:* Give verbal praise to those children who follow skill components. Teacher can read aloud a good picture book.

   E. *Discussion:* Discuss difficulties of not always doing what the rest of a group does.

6. **Practice:** Make "Peer Pressure Cards" using the situations on the accompanying activity sheet, "Decisions, Decisions," and others. Place the cards in a container and call upon children to reach in and select a card. Teacher can read it aloud. Children must select the appropriate answer.

7. **Independent Use:** Find out how someone at home has ignored peer pressure and has done what he or she needed to do. Have someone at home help you write it down and bring it to school.

8. **Continuation:** Teachers should stress the importance of making one's own choices and not just "going with the group."

CHILDREN'S LITERATURE

Carlson, Nancy. *Arnie and the Skateboard Gang.* New York: Viking.

Polacco, Patricia. *Babushka's Doll.* New York: Simon & Schuster, 1990.

Name _____   Date _____

DECISIONS, DECISIONS

?????????????????????????????

Each day we have to make decisions! Read the 3 sentences below and <u>underline</u> the BEST decision in each case. Discuss this in class.

?????????????????????????????

1. Mother needs bread from the store now. The gang wants to leave for the show in five minutes. What should you do?

    Tell mom the store is closed.

    Tell the gang you are sick.

    Get the bread and see if you can catch up with the gang.

_____

2. Bill is playing with baby brother. All the guys come by with their bats and balls. They want him to pitch for the big game. Baby can't go to the ball field. What should Bill do?

    Push baby down and make him cry.

    Tell the guys he'll play when baby is napping.

    Take baby to the ball field.

SOCIAL SKILL

Resisting Negative Pressure

Behavioral Objective: The children will say no when pressured by peers to do something they don't want to do.

Directed Lesson:

1. **Establish the Need:** Teacher initiates a discussion about the relevance and benefits of the skill. Children need to learn that they have choices in selecting actions that can either help them or hurt them. Children need to know that they have options in dealing with peer pressure. They must be made to understand that when someone is trying to get them to do something wrong, that person is not a friend. If children feel good enough about themselves and are secure, they can overcome this type of peer pressure.

2. **Introduction:** Read this story to the class:

   "Susan was a new girl in _____ school. She was assigned to Mr. Jones' second grade room. The teacher introduced her and Susan told the class some facts about herself. Mr. Jones seated Susan next to Ellen. Unfortunately, Ellen was the type of child who got into trouble frequently. During lunch, Ellen and Susan sat and talked. Susan was very happy to have made a friend. Then a few of Ellen's friends came over to get her to join them. They had decided to leave the school playground, which was against the rules. They wanted Susan to come with them too. She knew it was wrong, but Ellen said that if she didn't come, she wouldn't be her friend."

   Problem: What should Susan do? Why?

3. **Identify the Skill Components:** (List on board before class.)

   1. Think about what other children want you to do.
   2. What could happen if you do it?
   3. Decide if it is wrong.
   4. If it is, say *no* in a nice way.
   5. If asked, tell why you decided not to do it.

4. **Model the Skill:** The teacher models the skill steps by pretending to be a student and having a group of children pressure him/her to do something wrong (e.g., drawing on the board).

5. **Behavioral Rehearsal:**

   A. *Selection:* Teacher selects three pairs of students to role play.

B. *Role Play:* Students role play the following three situations:
1. Peer pressure to cheat on a test.
2. Peer pressure to destroy school property (e.g., desk).
3. Peer pressure to take someone's lunch.

C. *Completion:* After each role play, reinforce correct behavior, identify inappropriate behaviors, and reenact role play with corrections. If there are no corrections, role play is complete.

D. *Reinforcers:* verbal encouragement by teacher and the rest of class. Stickers for good role plays.

E. *Discussion:* Have the class discuss the role plays and the corrections that had to be made. Ask the students what problems might arise when trying to deal with peer pressure. Ask for suggestions on how to handle these problems. Discuss the consequences of not being able to say no when you don't want to do something.

6. ***Practice:*** Have children complete the following activity sheet, "Scrambled Answers."

7. ***Independent Use:*** Have students write down incidents outside the classroom where they had to deal with peer pressure. Write about how they were able to say no and how the others reacted to the *no.*

8. ***Continuation:*** Teachers should continue pointing out the need for this skill as related situations arise.

CHILDREN'S LITERATURE

Bunting, Eve. *The Man Who Could Call Down Owls.* New York: Macmillan (Atheneum), 1994.

Kline, Suzy. *Song Lee in Room Two B.* New York: Viking Children's Books, 1993.

Name_____ Date _____

SCRAMBLED ANSWERS

Directions: Read the questions and put the answers in the correct order.

Let's break this glass bowl.

NO! It's wrong!

1.   Will you sneak out of school with us?

    to   trouble   No,   in   don't   get   I   want

    _____

2.   Will you help us take money out of that purse?

    stealing   No,   wrong   is

    _____

3.   Will you help us trip that boy when he walks by?

    want   anyone   No,   don't   I   hurt   to

    _____

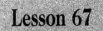
SOCIAL SKILL

Saying NO to Doing Wrong

Behavioral Objective: The children will say *no* when pressured by peers to do something they don't want to do.

Directed Lesson:

1. **Establish the Need:** Review the importance of being able to say no to things that you don't want to do. Discuss possible consequences if they don't have this skill. Stress that friends do not try to get you to do something wrong.

2. **Introduction:** Read this poem to the class:

> **We all have friends that we adore**
> **And that they like us we are sure**
> **We know they're friends because they care**
> **We know they're friends because they're fair!**
> **Then there are others who would lead us astray**
> **We must watch out or we will pay**
> **They'll try to get us to do wrong**
> **So with these people we don't belong!**
> **Say *no* to things you see are bad**
> **And you will end up being glad.**

3. **Identify the Skill Components:** (List on board before class.)

   1. Think about what other children want you to do.
   2. Decide what could happen if you do it.
   3. Decide if it is wrong to do.
   4. If it is wrong, say *no* in a nice way.
   5. If asked, tell why you decided not to do it.

4. **Model the Skill:** The teacher models the skill steps by pretending to be a student, and having a group of students try to get him/her to do something wrong (e.g., copy someone's homework).

5. **Behavioral Rehearsal:**

   A. *Selection:* Teacher selects students as needed and as time allows.

   B. *Role Play:* Students role play situations that were written for the previous lesson's independent use.

C. *Completion:* After each role play, reinforce correct behavior, identify inappropriate behaviors, and reenact role play with corrections. If there are no corrections, role play is complete.

D. *Reinforcers:* verbal praise by teacher and students; certificates for being able to withstand peer pressure. Have students give themselves a round of applause.

E. *Discussion:* Lead the group in a discussion of the role plays and what errors were made. Ask the students how they would handle the same type of peer pressure. What kind of difficulties have they had when saying no to other children? What kinds of things were said to them to persuade them to do something wrong?

6. **Practice:** Have children complete the following activity sheet, "The Answer Is 'NO'." The students must write how they would say no to someone trying to make them do something wrong. They must also write the reasons why they won't do it.

7. **Independent Use:** Keep a diary of incidents of peer pressure and how each one was dealt with. Try to write the exact words that were used to try to convince you to do something wrong and what you said.

8. **Continuation:** Teachers should remind children that true friends do not try to get us to do things that are wrong.

CHILDREN'S LITERATURE

Schecter, Ellen. *The Boy Who Cried Wolf.* New York: Bantam, 1994.

Wild, Jocelyn. Florence and Eric Take the Cake. New York: Puffin Books, 1990.

Name _____   Date _____

THE ANSWER IS "NO"

Directions: Write what you would say to someone trying to get you to do something that you don't want to do. Give the reason why you won't do it.

Problem: A few children from your class want you to get into a stranger's car.

Say: _____

Why: _____

Problem: A friend wants you to take money out of your mother's dresser drawer.

Say: _____

Why: _____

Problem: Some third graders want you to leave school with them during lunch.

Say: _____

Why: _____

SOCIAL SKILL

Avoiding a Wrong Choice

Behavioral Objective: The children will avoid making a wrong choice when encouraged by a peer.

Directed Lesson:

1. **Establish the Need:** Teacher will initiate a discussion about knowing right from wrong and choosing to do the right thing. Ask students to give you their ideas. **"What are some things which are wrong to do? What if someone tried to get you to steal? What might happen to you if you do go along and say yes to a wrong doing? Would you be grounded, sent to a detention home, or possibly jailed?"**

2. **Introduction:** **"David, I'm glad you didn't lie about breaking the glass when Liz told you to. I'm glad you know that you should tell the truth."**

3. **Identify the Skill Components:** (List on board before class.)

      1. Decide what is wrong to do.
      2. Decide why it is wrong to do.
      3. Learn to say *no,* if it is wrong to do.
      4. Walk away.

4. **Model the Skill:** Teacher will model the skill by using examples of saying no if it is wrong (e.g., steal a pencil that belongs to Joe, chase and kick Mrs. Smith's cat).

5. **Behavioral Rehearsal:**

      A. *Selection:* Teacher selects four pairs of children to role play.

      B. *Role Play:*
      1. Steal a game from the classroom.
      2. Ignore the new boy in class.
      3. Trick or play a joke on somebody.
      4. Steal Judy's new book bag.

      C. *Completion:* After each role play, reinforce correct behavior, identify inappropriate behaviors, and reenact role play with corrections. If there are no corrections, role play is complete.

    D. *Reinforcers:*

        1. **"Alex, you did the right thing. Thank you."**

        2. **"Good job, lets try the next role play."**

        3. **"Very good, smile."**

    E. *Discussion:* Have children discuss role plays. Which one did you like best? What are some things you learned from the lesson?

6. **Practice:** Complete and share the following activity sheet, "Meet Wally the Whale."

7. **Independent Use:** Share times when you said no to a wrong doing at home or neighborhood.

8. **Continuation:** As related situations arise, teachers should point out that each of us can choose what we do. If we know something to be wrong, we should simply not do it.

CHILDREN'S LITERATURE

Kline, Suzy. *Herbie Jones and the Birthday Showdown.* New York: Putnam, 1993.

Turkle, Brinton. *Obadiah the Bold.* New York: Puffin Books, 1977.

Name

Date

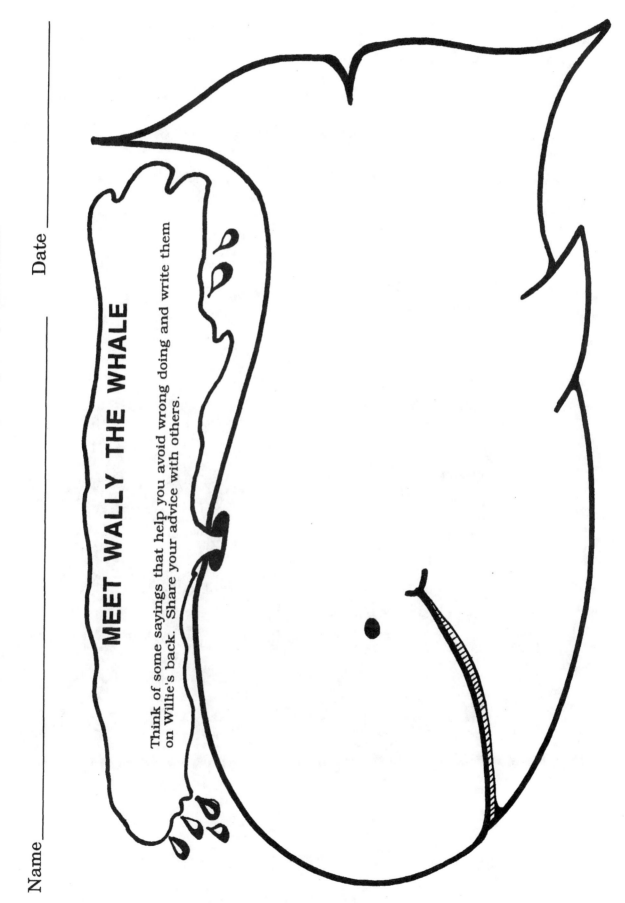

MEET WALLY THE WHALE

Think of some sayings that help you avoid wrong doing and write them on Willie's back. Share your advice with others.

Part I presents 21 social skills-related topics on cards for teacher-led class discussions during Circle Time. Each topic can be introduced once before studying a particular skill, such as listening, and later after the lesson, to assess children's learning.

NOTE: The topics are printed in the form of discussion cards which can be photocopied and cut out for use at the appropriate time.

SOCIAL SKILLS TASK REVIEW

Part I

Why are social skills important?

Social skills are important because their frequent use and application determines how well we get along with other people.

What are they?

respect for others	*kindness*
listening	*politeness*
following directions	*self-control*
sharing	*cooperation*
consideration	*patience*
caring	*problem solving*
accepting change	*conflict solving peacefully*

Listening is important because . . .

Listening is important because if we do not listen when other people speak to us, we will never learn what they are telling us or know how to do something they may be showing us.

We need to listen carefully at these times:

Fire drill
When teacher gives a listen signal
When teacher gives directions
Any time teacher or family have to say something

Completing assignments is important because . . .

It is important to finish any job that you choose or are given in order to learn how to do things and how to do them well.

Discuss the importance of finishing things we start. The format can be, "What would happen if . . . . "

- the road was only half finished
- the school bus had a flat tire that wasn't fixed
- the pizza was only half cooked, etc.

Why is it important to pay attention and not let other things distract you?

It is important to pay attention to what we are doing so that we can finish our work and learn how to do things.

What are we learning at school?

- how to paint
- how to put things away
- how to sit quietly and listen to a story, etc.
- how to make friends
- how to solve problems (conflicts) peacefully
- how to be helpful to others
- how to use magic courtesy words

It is important to follow instructions and directions because . . .

It is important to follow directions or instructions from your teacher or parents in order to prevent mistakes or accidents and to learn how to do things correctly and safely.

Why do we *walk* indoors and *run* outdoors?

Whose advice do you trust? Why?

Eg. I trust my mother's/father's/other relative's advice because she/he loves me and has my best interests at heart.

What advice do we give to someone who is

- crossing the street
- holding a pet
- being called by a stranger
- being talked to by a stranger, etc.

How do you settle conflicts without violence?

Eg. **We can talk about the problem and try to reach a compromise.**

We can ask someone else to listen to both sides of the conflict and tell us what they think is fair.

One of us can give in to the other or negotiate a different solution.

How can you avoid getting into a fight?

Eg. **I can avoid getting into a fight by controlling my anger.**

I can stop and count to ten when I feel myself growing very angry.

I can tell my teacher/relative about the problem instead of fighting.

It takes a lot of practice to learn to handle conflicts constructively. Let's try these things today:

(1) **Think before you speak.**

(2) **Speak in a quiet voice no matter how angry you may feel inside.**

Why is it important to be a good sport and accept consequences in a graceful manner?

Eg.　**It shows that you are a good sport.**

It sets a good example for others.

It makes you a better person.

It keeps you from fighting and getting hurt.

It teaches you to follow the rules.

How do you react when you fail at something?

Eg.　**I feel disappointed and frustrated.**

I promise myself that I will try again and succeed the next time.

I am embarrassed.

I will try to learn from failing not to fail again.

What we think about ourselves is very important. What do you *think* when someone tells you that you did a very good job?

Eg.　**I think they are complimenting me on my good work.**

I think they are encouraging me to keep up the good work.

I think I will try harder to do good work.

I think . . .

How do you *feel* when someone tells you that you did a very good job?

Eg. **I feel proud of myself.**

I feel good about myself.

I feel happy that my work pleases them.

I feel . . .

How can we show understanding of another's feelings?

Eg. **When someone is hurt we can . . .**

When someone is crying we can . . .

When someone falls down we can . . .

When someone spills something we can . . .

It helps to talk over feelings with other people you trust. If you felt bad about something, who could you talk with?

Eg. **I could talk about it with my mom/dad because she/he would understand how I felt and help me feel less bad.**

Who else can we talk to? At home? At school?

How do you feel when you get a deserved compliment? How can we compliment others? Let's try. We can begin with the words:

"I like the way _____"

"I like it when _____"

It is important to ask permission politely if you want to borrow anything. Why? How can we put it into words and use the words today?

Eg. **It is important to ask permission politely to borrow someone else's property because the more polite you are, the more likely they will be to let you use it.**

Eg. "May I use the blue crayon?"

"May I play with the blocks, too?"

"May I . . .

Suppose we had a day when five of us felt angry. What could we do to try to make it a good day?

Eg. **We could ask the five angry children to explain their feelings and see if there is some way to help them feel less angry.**

We can	walk away	tap our toes ten times
	hum a tune	count to ten
	look at a book	etc.

When someone gets angry with you, what are some ways that you can deal with their anger?

Eg. **I can talk to the person in a quiet voice.**

I can avoid getting angry myself.

I can count to ten.

I can try to calm the person by talking.

I can try to negotiate.

What things make you angry?

Eg. **I get angry when someone takes my belongings without asking me.**

I get angry when someone pushes ahead of me in the line.

I get angry when someone cheats in a game.

OK. So we feel mad. How can we "use our words" to tell about the anger rather than using our body?

Eg. **We can say in a quiet voice what we think is wrong and what should be done to make it right. We should find a solution that pleases both sides.**

What is positive peer pressure?

Positive peer pressure is being asked by friends or others to do something that is all right to do and that you may enjoy doing.

Eg. **. . . to play a game of baseball**

. . . to have dinner at their house

. . . to go to the movies with them

How do I react to positive peer pressure?

Eg. **You may decide to do something if you are free and like doing it.**

You may say "No, thanks" if you have other more important or enjoyable things to do.

You may simply say "Yes, I'd like to do that."

What is negative peer pressure?

Negative peer pressure is being asked by friends or others to do something that is wrong to do or something you do not like to do.

Eg. **. . . to make fun of another child**

. . . to steal something that belongs to someone else

. . . to hurt an animal or another person

How do I react to negative peer pressure?

Eg. **You may just say "NO!" in a nice way.**

You may say, "Sorry, but I have other things to do."

You may tell them that you think it's the wrong thing to do and not for you.

How do you feel about violence?

Eg. **I think violence is wrong because it hurts others and doesn't solve any problems.**

I think violence only causes hatred and leads to more violence.

I think violence happens when people get too fearful and emotional and do not think before they act.

How do you feel about non-violence?

Eg. **I think non-violence is the only way to settle arguments and solve problems between people.**

I think non-violence is the only way to achieve real and lasting peace among people.

SOCIAL SKILLS TASK REVIEW   Part II

Directions: Display the following social skills related words on a colorful chart with a catchy title such as that used in the example on the following page.

Discuss one word with the children each day. Then review the words using a procedure such as one of these:

- Have children use a pointer, point to a word and explain what it means.

- Have a child point to a word and ask one of his/her classmates to tell what the word means.

- Give the meaning of a word and ask a child to point to the correct word.

Words	*Sample Explanation*
Social Skills	what we need to get along with others
Conflict	a disagreement in ideas or interests
Attitude	how we think and act about someone or something
Compromise	an agreement in which each side gives up some demands or desires
Listening	to pay attention to what others are saying
Self-Image	how we think and feel about ourself and our abilities
Values	what we and others think are important and desirable to have
Peer Pressure	what our friends and peers want us to do
Negative Peer Pressure	what our peers want us to do but what is not right to do
Violence	fighting, shooting, hitting and more
Non-Violence	discussing, talking quietly, and more

SOMETHING TO SING ABOUT

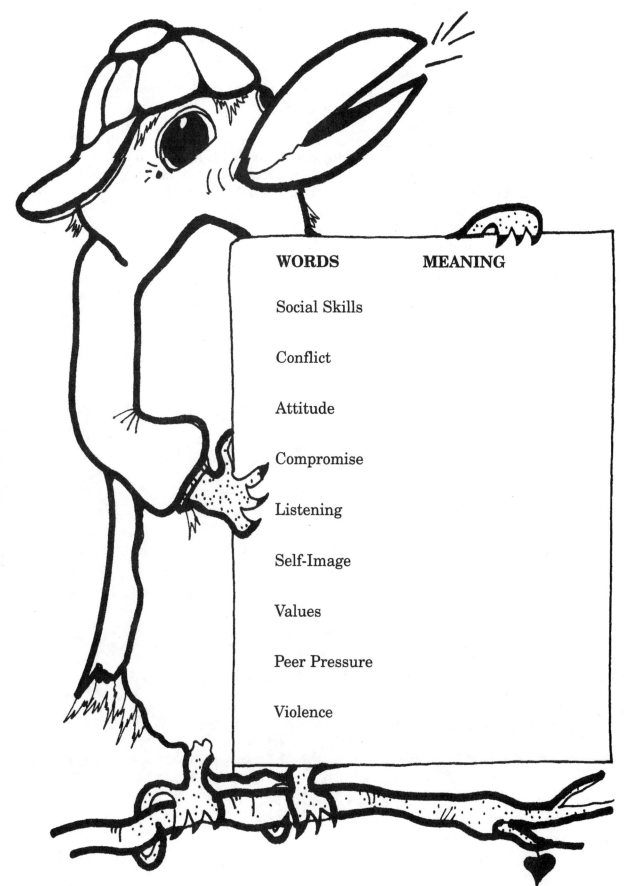

WORDS	MEANING
Social Skills	
Conflict	
Attitude	
Compromise	
Listening	
Self-Image	
Values	
Peer Pressure	
Violence	

SOCIAL SKILLS
FAMILY TRAINING BOOKLET

The following pages present a social skills family training booklet entitled "Partners in Social Skills: A Family Affair" preceded by a "Family Letter" that introduces the booklet and can be signed by each child. The letter provides a good way to involve parents in the social skills development program to coordinate home and classroom instruction.

NOTE: The letter and single pages of the booklet may be photocopied but only as many times as you need them for use with individual children, small groups, or an entire class. Reproduction of this material for an entire school system or for sale is strictly forbidden.

You may order copies of the booklets from The Center for Applied Research in Education. The minimum quantity is 20.

FAMILY LETTER

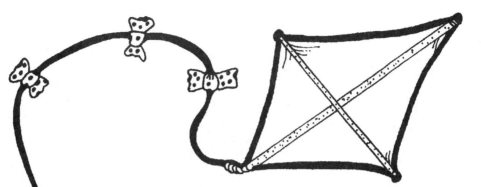

Dear Family:

In our classroom we are learning how to get along with each other; how to deal with our feelings; and how to deal with peer pressure. These are some of the things we are learning in our classroom lessons called Social Skills Training. We not only learn about these Social Skills, but also get a chance to practice those skills through role playing. After we role play the Social Skills in class, we discuss our role playing and practice the skills in school, at play and at home.

Your child,

We are Flying High

Partners in Social Skills

A Family Affair

 RUTH WELTMANN BEGUN, Editor
The Society for Prevention of Violence

ACKNOWLEDGMENTS

The Founders, Trustees, Members, Friends of the Society for Prevention of Violence (SPV), and many Foundations and Corporations sponsored the writing of this social skills training booklet, "Partners in Social Skills: A Family Affair." The objective of the booklet is to acquaint the family with social skills training and how it can be used to resolve conflicts and to improve the behavior, attitude, and responsibility of the children and other family members. The booklet will help the family reinforce Social Skills Training being taught in schools and can also be used by the family to teach social skills to pre-school children.

Credit for writing the booklet belongs to a group of teachers from the Cleveland (Ohio) Public Schools who worked under the guidance of Ruth Weltmann Begun, then Executive Director of SPV. All participants utilized their expertise and considered many variations of instructional approaches and ideas until a format for the publication was agreed upon.

INTRODUCTION

"Partners in Social Skills: A Family Affair" is a Social Skills Training resource guide to be used in a family setting. Social Skills Training helps a child to gain valuable skills such as self-esteem, self-control, respect for other persons, and responsibility for one's own actions. Such skills are very important for good family relationships, solid learning in school, and success all through life.

Some schools now offer Social Skills Training in their classrooms. For many children this supports what they are already learning at home. For many others, school is where they start to learn such skills. Many families today have single parents, or have two parents who both work, or have step-parents due to divorce and remarriage. All these changes put stress on families, and make parenting more challenging than in the past.

Today, the average child watches several hours of television each day, often without a parent or other adult present. TV scenes of violence or other harmful conduct can easily misguide young children.

This guide is designed to help parents in several ways:

(1) To introduce Social Skills Training to parents, and show them how this is already taught in some schools.

(2) To present some Social Skills Training activities that can be done at home.

(3) To encourage parents to apply this training with all of their children, even preschoolers.

(4) To remind parents that, no matter how much they may sometimes doubt it, *they* are the most important teachers in their children's lives.

The love, example, and guidance of parents and other adult family members can indeed make the difference for a child. He or she can learn, with their help, to respect others, make wise decisions, avoid violence, and become a successful and productive citizen as an adult.

Along the way, practicing the Social Skills included here should help the family enjoy a happier and less stressful home life.

THE SOCIAL SKILLS SONG
(Tune: "Mary Had a Little Lamb")

WE CAN USE OUR SOCIAL SKILLS
SOCIAL SKILLS, SOCIAL SKILLS
WE CAN USE OUR SOCIAL SKILLS
AS WE SPREAD OUR GOOD WILL

EVERY DAY IN EVERY WAY
EVERY WAY, EVERY WAY
EVERY DAY IN EVERY WAY
OUR CHARACTER WE BUILD

S elf-image improved
O nly giving compliments
C ompleting tasks
I gnoring distractions
A nger dealt with
L ess aggression

S eatwork and homework done
K eep following classroom rules
I gnoring teasing
L eave a troublesome situation
L earning to accept consequences
S taying out of fights

1. Compliments
2. Asking Permission
3. Disciplinary Strategies
4. Respect for Others
5. Self-Respect
6. Improving Self-Image
7. Feelings
8. Accepting Consequences
9. Accepting Failure
10. Setting Goals
11. Dealing with Prejudice
12. Dealing with Anger
13. Peer Pressure
14. Problem Solving

OUR FAMILY SOCIAL SKILLS TRAINING CHECKLIST

DIRECTIONS: Please fill out this checklist as a family before starting to read this book. Answer the way your family really feels by filling in the faces. There are no right or wrong answers.

This will help your family understand the need to practice Social Skills Training in your home.

Almost Always	Sometimes	Almost Never
☺	😐	☹

		Almost Always	Sometimes	Almost Never
1.	Do we understand and follow when directions are given?	☺	😐	☹
2.	Do we know and follow the rules in our home?	☺	😐	☹
3.	Do we listen to adults in authority?	☺	😐	☹
4.	Do we finish our household jobs?	☺	😐	☹
5.	Do we take our finished homework to school the next day?	☺	😐	☹
6.	Do we finish our housework even when others are not doing their share?	☺	😐	☹
7.	Do we keep busy and quiet when waiting for our parent's attention?	☺	😐	☹
8.	Do we find something quiet and helpful to do when we have free time?	☺	😐	☹
9.	Do we deal with anger in a way that won't hurt others?	☺	😐	☹
10.	Do we stay in control when somebody teases us?	☺	😐	☹
11.	Do we think of ways other than fighting to handle our problems?	☺	😐	☹
12.	Do we avoid fighting when someone threatens or hits us?	☺	😐	☹
13.	Do we accept the consequences when we do something we shouldn't?	☺	😐	☹
14.	Do we tell others that we like something nice about them or do something nice for them?	☺	😐	☹
15.	Do we say and do nice things for ourselves when we have earned it?	☺	😐	☹

HELPFUL HINTS FOR USING THIS BOOK

1. Set aside quiet time and space.

2. Involve all family members.

3. Discussions should be friendly, positive and open.

4. Listen to each member's comments.

5. Criticism should be done in a positive and peaceful way.

6. All family members should work on being good role models.

BE A ROLE MODEL FOR YOUR CHILD

- Let your child see you read. Visit the library with your child on a regular basis. At home, provide a quiet, well-lighted space for your child to study and read.

- Don't leave your children alone for long periods of time. Let your child know where and how to reach you. Leave your child with a happy feeling.

- Use kind and supportive words with your child. Unkind words can hurt as much as, or even more than, physical punishment.

- When resolving disputes or conflicts in the family, do your best to stay calm and in control of yourself.

- Beginning with yourself, make all family members responsible for keeping themselves and the house clean.

- Show your child how to "just say no" by your *own* saying no to drugs and other harmful activities.

- Remember that your child is learning from you, not only when you are telling him or her what to do, but *all* the time, by your example.

Family Activity Page

Toot Your Own Horn

Write or draw five things you can do well at home, at work, at school or at play.

FOURTEEN SELECTED SOCIAL SKILLS

The following pages contain fourteen selected Social Skills that have been taken from the "Social Skills Curriculum Activities Library" published by The Center for Applied Research in Education. Each skill is followed by skill activities. It is suggested that these activities can be done with all the family to develop the skill.

FAMILY SOCIAL SKILLS

Skill No. 1:   **Giving Compliments:**

Compliments mean saying something nice that makes someone else feel good.

Do these skill activities with your family:

1. Select someone to give a compliment.
2. Think of a compliment that is pleasing and truthful.
3. Say the compliment in a pleasant way.

Skill No. 2:   **Asking Permission:**

Permission means giving consent.

Do these skill activities with your family.

1. Ask if you may borrow something.
2. Do not take the item if the answer is no.
3. If given permission, be careful with the item and return it in good condition.
4. Say "thank you."

11

Skill No. 3:   **Disciplinary Strategies:**

Discipline is training and conduct that develops self-control.

Do these skill activities with your family:

1. Develop rules and consequences for family members.
2. Encourage all members to follow the rules.
3. Evaluate and change the rules when needed.

Skill No. 4:   **Respect for Others:**

Respect means to be kind and courteous to others.

Do these skill activities with your family:

1. Use the words "may I" when asking someone for something.
2. Use "please" and "thank you" when asking and receiving help.
3. Practice using these words often.

Skill No. 5:   **Using Self-Control:**

Self-control is remaining calm under stress and excitement.

Do these skill activities with your family:

1. Stop and think about the situation that was causing stress to you and made you excited.
2. Count to ten while trying to remain calm.
3. Decide what you will do next.
4. Do it in a peaceful manner.

Skill No. 6:   **Improving Self-Image:**

Self-image is how you see yourself.

Do these skill activities with your family:

1. Think of something you like about yourself.
2. Share it with your family members.
3. Discuss more ways you are special.

Skill No. 7:   **Expressing Feelings:**

Some feeling words are: happy, sad, angry, embarrassed, depressed, proud, guilty, frustrated and many more.

Do these skill activities with your family:

1. Listen to the tone of voice, watch facial expressions and body gestures to understand the feelings in a message.
2. Ask the speaker if you understood his or her feelings correctly.

Skill No. 8:   Accepting Consequences:

Accepting the results of one's own actions without complaining.

Do these skill activities with your family:

    1. Decide if what you did was wrong.
    2. Admit what you did was wrong.
    3. Try to explain why you did it.
    4. Accept the punishment without complaint.

Skill No. 9:   Reacting to Failure:

Failure is an unsuccessful attempt to achieve a goal.

Do these skill activities with your family.

    1. Discuss what it means to fail.
    2. Decide why you failed.
    3. Accept the failure.
    4. Make a new plan to avoid making any similar mistakes.

Skill No. 10:   Setting Goals:

Goals are plans of action which can be achieved.

Do these skill activities with your family:

1. Think about things that need to be done at home or school.
2. Choose a goal and decide how it can be reached.
3. Reward yourself when you have reached your goal.

Skill No. 11:   Dealing with Prejudice:

Prejudice is caused because of differences existing between people which are not acceptable to you.

Do these skill activities with your family:

1. Discuss individual physical differences.
2. Discuss likenesses.
3. Treat everyone equally and with respect.
4. Discuss positive qualities and include everyone in your activities.

Skill No. 12:   Dealing with Anger:

Everyone gets angry but anger must be resolved in a peaceful, verbal and non-physical manner.

Do these skill activities with your family:

1. Stop and think about how you feel.
2. Think of non-threatening ways to handle your anger.
3. Choose an action that will resolve the conflict.
4. If there is no other choice, walk away.

Skill No. 13:   **Dealing with Peer Pressure:**

Peer Pressure means that pressure is being strongly forced on you by friends, to do something you might or might not want to do. You might decide that what they want you to do is right or wrong.

> We all have friends that we adore
> And that they like us we are sure
> We know they're friends because they care
> We know they're friends because they're fair
> Then there are others that are fakes
> We must watch out for our own sakes
> They'll try to get us to do much wrong
> So with these people we don't belong
> Say no to things you see are bad
> And for yourself you'll be glad
> Friends won't ask us to misbehave
> If you say no, we'll rave and rave.

After reading the poem do these skill activities with your family:

1. Decide if what your friends want you to do is right or wrong. If it seems wrong, consider the consequences. Don't join activities which hurt, damage others, or yourself. If caught you might be **imprisoned and penalized**. Say "NO" to drugs, alcohol and early sex. They will harm you.
2. Make a decision you can live with.
3. Think of other activities the group could participate in that are acceptable.

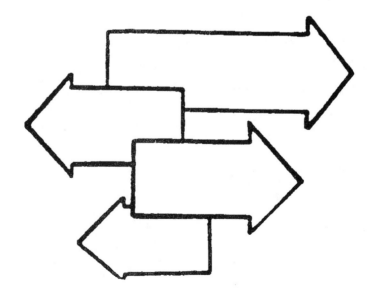

Skill No. 14:   Problem Solving:

There are many ways to solve a problem and make a decision. All possibilities should be considered to find the best solution.

Do these skill activities with your family:

1. State the problem and list ways it can be solved.
2. Select and try one of the choices.
3. If it does not work try another solution until you find the best one.

Family Activity Page

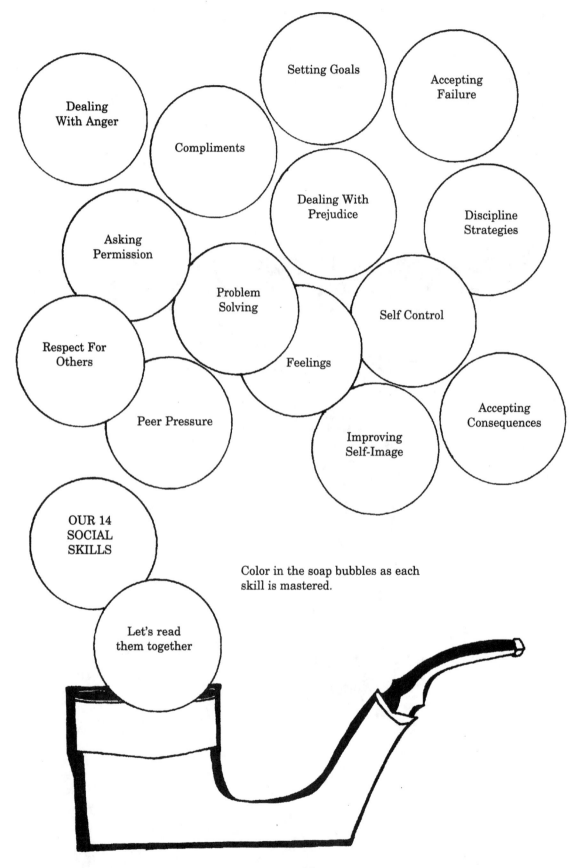

Setting Goals

Accepting Failure

Dealing With Anger

Compliments

Dealing With Prejudice

Discipline Strategies

Asking Permission

Problem Solving

Self Control

Respect For Others

Feelings

Peer Pressure

Improving Self-Image

Accepting Consequences

OUR 14 SOCIAL SKILLS

Color in the soap bubbles as each skill is mastered.

Let's read them together

18

"MIRROR, MIRROR" POEM

Read the poem. Think of someone to compliment. Draw their picture, and write the compliment underneath.

Mirror, mirror on the wall
Give a compliment, and that's not all
Make it nice and make it kind
A deserving person is not hard to find.

Family Activity Page, Certificate

Use this certificate to reward family members for proper use of social skills.

BEAR-R-Y GOOD FOR YOU!

NAME:

SKILLS:

DATE:

Use this certificate to reward family members for proper use of social skills.

FAMILY TIME—GROUP DISCUSSIONS

Directions to Family: Please set aside ten to fifteen minutes daily to discuss the following questions with family members. During the family discussion be sure to listen to each other. Every family member should be encouraged to give input. Refer to the Social Skills listed in this book.

1. What Social Skills did you learn today?

2. What Social Skills did you use today?

3. What Social Skills did we use within our home?

4. What Social Skills did you use in solving a personal conflict?

5. Did you use courtesy words like "please" and "thank you" when requesting and receiving assistance?

6. What did you do today that made you feel proud?

7. What assignments including household chores did you complete today?

8. Were there any consequences that were difficult for you to accept?

9. How did you show respect for someone today?

10. Did you compliment someone today? How did this make you feel? How did this make the other person feel?

11. Which Social Skill will be our goal to work on tomorrow?

WHAT MAKES YOU HAPPY?

Directions to Family: It is suggested that all family members take part in this activity. Each member may list or draw three things that make them happy. (You may want to use additional paper.)

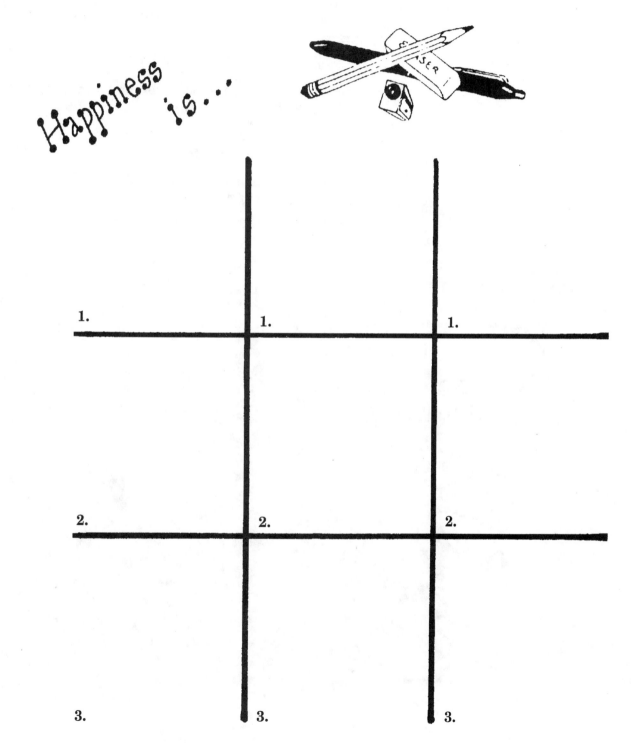

PARENT-TEACHER COMMUNICATION

1. Make appointments to visit your child's teacher or teachers.

2. Ask about any new changes in the curriculum.

3. Become a part of the PTA and other school related groups.

4. Get to know your principal.

5. Become aware of Parent Conference days, and become aware of your child's progress.

6. Learn about the community resources that can be of service to you and your family.

7. Feel free to spend time in your child's classroom to see how Social Skills Training is taught.

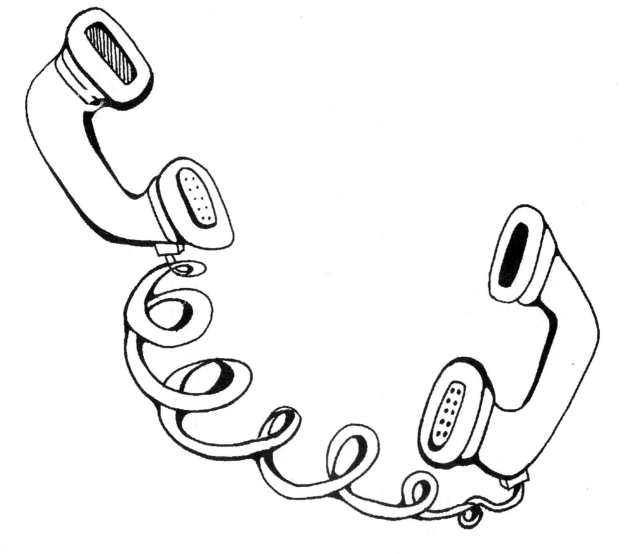

After working on social skills, Mr. and Mrs. Mouse took their family on a cookout.

Activity Color Page, Part II

Tommy Mouse and his sister were happy about the cookout. They watched their manners and talked about what fun they had making it a family affair. They all agreed to work, play, and respect one another. How about your family members?

OUR FAMILY SOCIAL SKILLS TRAINING CHECKLIST

DIRECTIONS: Please fill out this reaction sheet as a family, when you have completed this book.

This may be used to help your family better understand what Social Skills need to be reinforced within the home.

Almost Always ☺	Sometimes 😐	Almost Never ☹

		Almost Always	Sometimes	Almost Never
1.	Do we understand and follow when directions are given?	☺	😐	☹
2.	Do we know and follow the rules in our home?	☺	😐	☹
3.	Do we listen to adults in authority?	☺	😐	☹
4.	Do we finish our household jobs?	☺	😐	☹
5.	Do we take our finished homework to school the next day?	☺	😐	☹
6.	Do we finish our housework even when others are not doing their share?	☺	😐	☹
7.	Do we keep busy and quiet when waiting for our parent's attention?	☺	😐	☹
8.	Do we find something quiet and helpful to do when we have free time?	☺	😐	☹
9.	Do we deal with anger in a way that won't hurt others?	☺	😐	☹
10.	Do we stay in control when somebody teases us?	☺	😐	☹
11.	Do we think of ways other than fighting to handle our problems?	☺	😐	☹
12.	Do we avoid fighting when someone threatens or hits us?	☺	😐	☹
13.	Do we accept the consequences when we do something we shouldn't?	☺	😐	☹
14.	Do we tell others that we like something nice about them or do something nice for them?	☺	😐	☹
15.	Do we say and do nice things for ourselves when we have earned it?	☺	😐	☹

GUIDELINES FOR CARING PARENTS

I.   How your children learn to act depends on what they are taught—and YOU are their most important teacher.

II.   Your children will learn more from watching what you do than from listening to what you say to do.

III.   Remember that you were once a child, and treat your children with patience and understanding.

IV.   Be fair, be consistent, and respect your children as you would have them respect you.

V.   Stay close to your children, but give them room to learn from their own experiences and to think for themselves.

VI.   Show your children things in life that are beautiful, and show that you appreciate these things.

VII.   Love your children with all your heart, your mind and your strength, and everything else will follow.

Dedicated to all family members who accept the challenge of helping each other develop into mature, healthy, stable, responsible and productive citizens.